THE
GRANDMA
FORCE

How Grandmothers are Changing
Grandchildren, Families, and Themselves

HARRIET HODGSON BS,MA

Virginia

Published in the United States by WriteLife Publishing (an imprint of Boutique of Quality Books Publishing Company, Inc.)
www.writelife.com

Printed in the United States of America.
Library of Congress Control Number: 2019940375

978-1-60808-218-6 (p)
978-1-60808-219-3 (e)

Book design by Robin Krauss, www.bookformatters.com
Cover design by Rebecca Lown, https://www.rebeccalowndesign.com/
Author photo by Haley Earley, Independent Photographer

First editor: Olivia Swenson
Second editor: Caleb Guard

Praise for Harriet Hodgson and
The Grandma Force

"Harriet Hodson is a force. Don't miss this timely book about a group with quiet power."

> — Neil Chethik author of *FatherLoss*
> and Executive Director of the Carnegie Center

"In this book, seasoned writer, researcher, and speaker Harriet Hodgson provides inspiration and wise direction to grandmothers of all ages. With a wide variety of valuable ideas from creating a mission statement to becoming a better communicator to taking care of yourself and becoming an advocate for those you love, you will be reminded that wise, dedicated grandmas not only leave an important legacy but can change the world."

> — Linda Eyre, New York Times Best Selling
> Author of *Grandmothering*

"I dare say, I've read most every book on grandparenting. *The Grandma Force* is my dream come true book for today's grandmother. Harriet Hodgson has done a masterful job sharing her personal grandparent wisdom, plus she speaks from her hard-earned experience raising her twin grandchildren after the tragic deaths of their parents. What makes this book such a delight to read is how the author beautifully gathered insights and wisdom from the best experts and resources and wrapped them up into one "must read" book for grandparents. If you are an experienced or veteran grandparent, *The Grandma Force* has something for you."

> — Christine Crosby, Editorial Director for
> *GRAND* magazine

"*The Grandma Force* is the most comprehensive book on grandparenting I've ever read. Harriet has researched and referenced every aspect of the grandma relationship and written an inspiring guide for grandmas who want to build a loving, lifelong bond with their grandchildren. Grandmas at every stage will benefit from this book!

— Donne Davis, Found/Director of
www.thegagasisterhood.com

"Harriet Hodgson really hit the nail on the head about writing your grandma mission statement. I find it very useful to remember and it is great to review this periodically and update it. The section on self-care is also very helpful because grandmothers, mothers, and women in general tend to push their own needs to the back burner. *The Grandma Force* helps us remember that by taking care of ourselves we can be the best grandmother we can be.

— Christine Wasilewski

To the grandmothers of the world,
who shape children's lives,
care for families,
share talents and skills,
improve communities,
and give endless love.
The world is better because of you.

CONTENTS

ABOUT THIS BOOK

The Grandma Force is an informal, global, multi-cultural network of grandmothers working singly and together to better the lives of grandchildren.

The purpose of this book is to make you aware of your talents, strengths, and knowledge, and to spur action. One person can make a difference, and that person is you. Each chapter emphasizes how important you are to your family and grandchild. This book has many helpful features that make reading easier and faster.

- First, it's written in a conversational style.
- The sub-topics of each chapter are listed on the beginning page.
- Bold headings help you track the sub-topics in each chapter.
- Real-life stories are blended with applicable research findings.
- Key points are highlighted within the text.
- Research resources are listed at the end of each chapter.
- Each chapter contains information you can use.

We are living in a complex, conflicted, scary time in history. Waiting for things to improve can be risky, so many grandmas have become proactive, and their voices are being heard. Every grandma has talents, education, and wisdom to share. These traits add up to power. You have the power to make a difference. Use your power for the good of your grandchild and other grandchildren in the community. Life has given you one of its greatest gifts—the sheer joy of being a grandma. Welcome to the Grandma Force!

PREFACE

I'm crazy about kids and always wanted to be a mother and grandmother. In 1992 my elder daughter, Helen, gave birth to fraternal twins. Excited as I was, the grandma role wasn't an instant fit, and I adapted to it gradually. Your experience may be like mine. Each grandma creates the role for herself, in her own time, and in her own way. The Grandma Force is based on my experience as a grandmother and guardian—a challenging, rewarding, hopeful journey that led me in new directions.

Becoming a grandma changed me.

When I became a grandma, my husband John and I lived in Stillwater, Minnesota, a historic river town founded in 1837. We loved Stillwater, but it was an hour-and-a-half drive to our daughter's home in Rochester, Minnesota. Long-distance grandparenting wasn't our choice, and all we could do was make the best of it. We saw the twins every two months or so and were always astonished at how much they had grown. How could this be?

A former teacher, I was pretty good about remembering kids' birthdays and holidays and choosing age-appropriate activities. I thought I was a keen observer too. From afar, Helen's family looked like a happy one, but the reality turned out to be different. Helen and her husband were having marital problems and divorced when the twins were about five years old. We provided emotional support for Helen and helped her move twice. Finally, she settled in Kasson, Minnesota, a rural town close to Rochester.

We had moved back to Rochester by then and John, a specialist in internal, preventive, and aviation medicine, returned to work at Mayo Clinic. Our lives settled into a routine. John was busy practicing medicine, and I was busy with writing projects. At the suggestion of a friend, Helen asked if she and the twins could come for dinner every Sunday so we could have more time together. It was an old-fashioned idea, and one that worked for us. Sunday dinners became special.

One summer evening as Helen was backing out of our driveway, she stuck her head out of the car window and called, "I forgot to tell you I made a will. You're listed as the twins' guardians. Is that okay?"

We said yes, waved goodbye, and didn't think any more about it. Who wanted to think about sad things on a glorious evening? The air smelled like mowed grass. Nearly Wild roses, a special variety with floppy petals, bloomed in the front garden. The sun was starting to go down and it would be dark soon. Nothing would happen to Helen, and life would be normal.

Helen's planning proved to be providential.

On a snowy Friday night in February of 2007, Helen died from the injuries she received in a car crash. Two days later, on the same weekend, my father-in-law (Pampa) succumbed to pneumonia. When I saw Helen's and Pampa's photos on the obituary page of the newspaper, I sobbed uncontrollably. Friends visited us and offered words of comfort. Still, life was dark, and became darker two months later when my brother, and only sibling, died of a heart attack. In November, the twins' father died from injuries he received in another car crash.

Four successive deaths were too much sorrow and too much pain.

Death wasn't new to me. My parents had died, relatives had died, friends had died, pets had died. I thought past grief experiences would help me cope with new grief. They only helped a little. The death of a child is like no other; I never felt such sorrow. Did I have the strength to grieve for multiple losses and raise teenagers? Unsure as I was, I was determined to find the strength I needed. The twins needed my love and support. I wouldn't fail Helen and I wouldn't fail myself.

The court followed the wording of Helen's will and appointed us as the twins' guardians and financial conservators. John and I divided our duties along traditional lines. I took care of home and school; he took care of finances and documents. We shepherded the twins through high school and they graduated with honors. We helped with college searches in a gentle, non-threatening way. When the twins were college students, I sent them care packages. Of all the goodies I sent, my granddaughter liked the homemade orange biscotti with chocolate chips best.

Seven years passed. During this time the twins became "our kids" and we became a grandfamily—a term created by AARP. Now I look back at this time of life with a sense of pride. We loved being grandparents then and still love being grandparents.

If you've been a grandma for several years, you know the joy it brings. If you're new at this grandma stuff, you are starting an amazing journey. Becoming a grandma opens a floodgate of memories. You may remember your child playing in the sandbox, feeding the dog from the table (a no-no), having noisy sleepovers with friends, learning to drive (and the first dent in the car), and dressing up for the prom. Memories like these made you realize, yet again, that time passes quickly. You anticipated and maybe vowed to make the most of the time you have with your grandkids.

Before I became a grandma, I thought motherhood was the starring role of life. I delivered two beautiful, healthy daughters and dreamed of bright futures for them. I treasured childhood markers, such as Helen taking her first steps holding onto the handle of a small wagon filled with colored blocks. Decades later, I can feel the joy of that moment and remember the tears that filled my eyes. I remember going over to Helen, hugging her, and saying, "You're walking!" This was an achievement for her and a change for us.

Irish poet John O'Donohue calls changes like these "thresholds." In in his book *To Bless the Space Between Us*, O'Donohue says life's changes make us ask about the threshold we're standing on now. Thresholds aren't simple boundaries; they are frontiers that divide different territories, rhythms, and atmospheres. Real frontiers can't be crossed "without the heart being passionately engaged and woken up." These words made me think about becoming a grandma.

The role was tentative at first, and I tried to understand how it fit into family dynamics and how to do it. What if I blew it? As the months passed, my confidence grew. I loved the twins fiercely and still love them fiercely. Although it's been years since the twins lived with us, people ask what became of them and wait eagerly for my reply. Unlike some grandparenting stories, ours has a happy ending, and I enjoy sharing how my grandson is going to medical school and my granddaughter is an independent photographer. When I talk about the twins, I always credit them for their success.

After the twins moved out of the house, John and I experienced the empty nest syndrome again. Only this time, it was worse. The house was quiet—too quiet—and I missed the twins' energy, conversation, and laughter. I remembered the time I asked my granddaughter to tell her brother dinner was ready. He was sitting at the desk in his bedroom at the top of the stairs. Instead of standing at the bottom of the stairs and calling her brother, she called him on her cell phone. "I can't believe you used a cell phone!" I exclaimed. My granddaughter burst out laughing.

I didn't understand the impact grandparenting had on me until I passed several thresholds. Today I see life more clearly. The family picture that began with a few brush strokes is colorful, vibrant, and complete. Others must see this picture because I'm constantly asked, "What would the twins have done without you?" I can't answer this question. All I can say is that being a grandma is the best thing I've ever done.

CHAPTER 1

The Contemporary Grandma

Grandma at a Crossroads
Mothers in the 1940s
Life During World War II
Then and Now
Caring for the Next Generation
Sharing Generational Skills

Grandparents used to be considered old, tired, and worn out. No more. Today's grandparents enjoy better health, stay physically active, volunteer in their communities, pursue new interests, and have longer lives. The American Grandparents Association (AGA) shared statistics of today's grandparents that paint a different picture than the stereotype: 33 percent of grandparents have been married twice, 15 percent have demonstrated for a cause, and 10 percent have tattoos.[1] Grandparents are even getting younger: the average age of a grandma is forty-eight, not old by modern standards.[2]

---

1 "Surprising Facts about Grandparents," American Grandparents Association (AGA).
2 "Surprising Facts about Grandparents," AGA.

Grandma at a Crossroads

In earlier decades, the mother of the family stayed home and took care of the children while the father worked outside the home. Today, both parents may work and, consequently, need reliable help for children. Grandma or Grandpa is often that helper, the one who changes diapers, fixes meals, drives kids to school, and reads to children. A grandparent is the one to call when a grandchild is ill. Grandparents may also contribute financially to the family.

For these reasons and more, grandparents are the foundation of the family—a support system, protective shield, calming influence, and source of love. Whether you are ready for these changes or not, today's grandparents are at a crossroads. Each grandparent can choose how their role as grandma or grandpa will be defined as they recognize their responsibilities and validate them in ways that empower all generations.

As a grandmother, I'd like to focus this book on grandmas. Whether you're a new or experienced grandma, the grandma role is always evolving. You need to decide what kind of grandma you want to be. You can be a quiet, uninvolved grandma, stay home and pursue your interests. Or you can be a proactive grandma, one who stands up for her beliefs, her beloved grandchild, helps the family, and works to improve the community. The choice is yours.

Let's take a brief look at yesterday's mothers and grandmas and how they lived, the challenges they faced, and how they responded to these challenges. I'll be sharing some of my own experiences and encourage you to think of your experiences. When I compare my life with my mother's life, I'm astonished at what she was able to accomplish with a limited education (she never graduated from high school), no funds, and no transportation. At the time, families had one car, if they had a car at all. We had one car, but my mother didn't know how to drive. Though she took driving lessons for a while, she stopped after she hit the front porch of our house.

My mother inspired me as a child and continues to inspire me. You may have similar feelings about your mother and grandmother. Looking at the roles women filled in the past may clarify your idea of the kind of grandma you want to be. This history may also give you perspective on the challenges you face as a grandma.

Mothers in the 1940s

Letters and phone calls were the main forms of communication when I was little. In Great Neck, a village on Long Island where my family lived (and it's still called a village), mail was delivered twice a day, once in the morning and again in the afternoon. We always looked forward to the mailman walking up our front steps. Double deliveries are unheard of today, and mail has become a rare form of communication. A thank-you note is even more rare.

My mother and her younger sister talked on the phone daily. Oddly, if my mother called her sister it was a local call, but if my aunt called my mother, it was a long-distance call. The clever Clifton sisters devised a plan. When my aunt wanted to talk to my mother, she dialed our phone number, let it ring three times, and hung up immediately. This was my mother's signal to call her back, and they talked on the phone for hours. They were very close and phone calls helped them maintain this relationship. People still rely on cell phones for communication today, though now the phones travel with them, and texting has often replaced conversation.

At the time, mothers were expected to stay home and manage the household. Certainly, there was lots of work to be done. Mother spent hours in the kitchen and wore an apron when she prepared meals. Since there were no mixes or meal kits, everything was made from scratch. Orange juice wasn't fresh or frozen, it was squeezed from oranges. My mother squeezed a bag of oranges every morning. A milk truck delivered milk and left it in an insulated box by the back door. Bread and other baked goods were delivered by a bakery truck.

Although Mom loved to bake and was an excellent baker, she bought cupcakes from the truck because it saved time. There were six in a box: two with vanilla frosting, two with chocolate, and two with strawberry. I loved them all.

Plates were smaller then, which reduced the serving sizes. Like all the families on the block, we had an ice box. Every few days an ice truck delivered a block of ice to our house. Graduating from an ice box to an electric refrigerator was a big deal, and my parents were excited about it. If I recall, a blue water pitcher came with the refrigerator. Plastic food storage bags hadn't been invented yet. Leftovers were wrapped in wax paper or stored in glass refrigerator dishes. These glass containers have made a comeback as people worried about the dangers of plastics, and I've seen them in discount stores and online.

There were no home electric dishwashers, and dishes were washed and dried by hand. What a concept!

Mothers had weekday clothes and good clothes, often called Sunday clothes. To save her good clothes, a mother wore a "house dress" while she cleaned. My mother had three house dresses, and they were all ugly. Socks with holes in them weren't thrown away. Instead, they were repaired with a darning egg (a large wooden egg with a handle), needle, and thread. Mom taught me how to darn socks. First, I covered the hole with perpendicular strands of thread, a task that required patience and concentration. Then I wove in a second set of threads perpendicular to the first. Darning socks was tedious work.

A mother who knew how to use a treadle-powered or electric sewing machine bought sewing patterns and made her own clothes and clothes for the family. Choosing sewing patterns could take hours. My mother acquired a used table-type sewing machine and made one dress for me. Considering it was her first effort, the dress fit well, and I wore it. I guess Mom didn't like sewing because she never made anything else. She closed the lid of the sewing machine table and it stayed closed. Today, old sewing patterns have become collectibles and are available online. I still have patterns from my home sewing days.

Entertainment was simple then—listening to the radio, playing cards, playing board games, reading magazines and books, going to the movies, gardening, and doing craft projects. My brother and I caught every episode of "Captain Midnight," "Jack Armstrong" and "The Shadow" on the radio. We were thrilled when the mailman delivered our genuine Captain Midnight decoder rings and looked forward to using them with the next program. It was a disappointing experience. After following the instructions and deciphering the code, which took longer than I thought, the message was "Tune in tomorrow," or something boring like that.

Black-and-white television was in its infancy, and few families had a set. My father sold industrial finishes to factories. One factory made television sets, and Dad was able to buy a set at a discount. We watched Phil Spitalny and his All-Girl Orchestra and stayed up late watching live theater productions. Long after my mother, brother, and I had gone to bed, Dad would stay up late and watch boxing matches.

Believe it or not, conversation was
a form of entertainment.

On summer evenings, folks in my neighborhood sat on their front porches, watched the fireflies come out, and told stories until it was time for bed. I caught fireflies in a jar. When I wasn't catching fireflies, I sat on our tiny porch with my parents and waited for the Good Humor man, who drove an ice cream truck around neighborhoods. The driver rang a set of windshield bells to let people know he was coming. Occasionally we bought ice cream from the truck, but most of the time we didn't because it was pricey.

Laundry was a labor-intensive task, and mothers usually did it on Monday. We had a wringer washing machine, a beast of an appliance with an open tub and wringer on top. Laundry was fed into the wringer to remove excess water. I was upstairs when my mother called, "Harriet, come here." Something about her voice alerted me. I ran down to the basement and discovered my mother's arm was caught in the wringer up to her elbow. Following her instructions, which Mom gave in an amazingly calm voice, I reversed the wringer and freed her arm. Thankfully, my mother wasn't severely injured, but the memory of this experience still makes me shudder.

Although clothes dryers were invented in 1930, they weren't readily available, and laundry was dried on a clothesline. Our clothesline ran from the back corner of the house, over the yard, to the corner of the garage. A canvas clothespin bag hung from the clothesline and stayed there in rain, sleet, and snow. Modesty existed back then, and my mother dried panties and bras in a pillow case so neighbors wouldn't see her "unmentionables." Modesty seems to have disappeared and nothing is unmentionable today.

Life During World War II

All family members—parents, children, grandparents, cousins, aunts, and uncles— were affected by World War II rationing.

The US government had three national programs: victory gardens, food canning, and knitting for the troops. Our victory garden was in an open field at the top of a hill. Some families marked off their plots with metal stakes and rope. People grew what they needed most: carrots, onions, potatoes, lettuce, cabbage, cucumbers, zucchini, and tomatoes. As the plants grew and matured, the field was transformed into a living quilt of produce. Tending a victory garden wasn't just a necessity; it was a social experience. Neighbors weeded and watered while they swapped stories about food rationing, the shortage of gas, and war developments.

One story was about a German submarine surfacing in Long Island Sound. I didn't know if the story was true. Decades later, I learned there were spies on Long Island.[3] Some German men who lived in the US returned to Germany for spy training that included creating explosives, building timers, and writing in code. After training, they returned to the states in a U-boat, which ran aground several times. They finally disembarked on a beach at the end of Long Island. The spies were dressed in German uniforms and had plans to blow up factories to slow

3 Michael Sheridan, "Secret Nazi Saboteurs Invaded Long Island During World War II, M15 Documents Reveal," *New York Daily News*, April 4, 2011.

war production. The bumbling spies were caught by a Coast Guard soldier.

Schools had air raid drills. I remember a drill at Lakeville Elementary School when I crouched by the furnace with my hands over my head. The teacher told me it was a fire drill, but I knew it wasn't. Air raids and spies were constantly on my mind. My brother assembled World War II plane models and hung them from his bedroom ceiling. When we played outside we usually played war, and I was always a Japanese soldier.

One evening I noticed ink spots on the bottom corner of the newspaper. I asked my mother if the different spots could be a code for enemy spies. She was shocked. Until that moment, I don't think my mother realized how aware I was of the war. Despite her assurances of no spies and no code, I continued to worry.

Sugar was in short supply and rationed. My husband still has his ration book, now a family artifact. I have my mother's cookbook, *The Victory Cook Book: Wartime Edition*, which contains substitutes for rationed ingredients and recipes for inexpensive wartime meals. Although I've never made the recipes, I read the book to get a sense of history. The chapter titled "How to Feed a Family of Five on $15 a Week" contains menus with lots of vegetables and little meat. Prune Whip, a gloppy brown dessert, was one of my mother's favorite recipes. When I sampled the dessert I grimaced, yet the courteous members of the bridge club complimented her on it.

Cookbooks included information about safe home canning methods[4]—the second government program. The US Department of Agriculture (USDA) Extension Services

---

4 Dr. Kelly A. Spring, "Food Rationing and Canning in World War II," National Women's History Museum.

published and distributed canning information. Victory gardens reached their peak in 1943 and so did canning. About four billion cans and jars of food were preserved that year.

My mother didn't can food, but she did grind the little beef we had into hamburger. The hand-crank grinder was bolted to a wooden stepstool. I didn't like the hamburger it produced because the grind was so large the hamburgers fell apart. When we had meat, the fat (such as bacon fat) was poured into a tin can and taken to the butcher. The government paid people by the pound for the fat, and it was used to make explosives. I couldn't understand how fat could be made into bombs. All I knew was that I was responsible for delivering cans of fat to the grocery store.

The third government program, "knitting for the boys," became an international program. Soldiers had barely grabbed their guns before wives and sweethearts grabbed knitting needles and yarn.[5] Elementary students, including my husband, learned to knit and made afghan squares. While machine knitting was more efficient, hand knitting kept women and children involved in war efforts. The American Red Cross was designated as the clearing agency and provided free patterns for sweaters, hats, mittens, and scarves. These patterns are still available online.

Although the nation was at war and worried about spies, a mother didn't lock the house. Neighbors took care of neighbors and watched each other's homes. When I walked to the grocery store, I greeted the neighbors I met by name. "Hello, Mrs. Smith." "Good morning, Mrs. Larson. What's Patty doing these days?" This is a sharp contrast to modern neighborhoods. Many families have no idea who lives next door or on the block. I've

---

5 Paula Becker, "Knitting for Victory—World War II," History Link.

lived in my present neighborhood for almost five years and still don't know all my neighbors.

When I was in high school, my career options included teacher, nurse, or secretary. World War II changed female employment forever. Women worked in factories, shipyards, and on farms. Posters of Rosie the Riveter, a fictitious symbol of working women, appeared coast to coast. Rosie wore a red bandana and above her face were the words, "We Can Do It!"

To my surprise, my mother went to work at the Sperry manufacturing plant near our home. In a few weeks, Mom changed from homemaker to factory worker and helped to assemble gyroscopes—devices used in navigation systems. She brought a gyroscope home to us (something she probably shouldn't have done), and I tried to spin it like a top. The gyroscope didn't spin and, much to my disappointment, fell over.

Dad was ambivalent about my mother having a job. Because he was the air raid warden for our block, he understood the need for her job and tolerated it. He was also glad for the extra income. After the war, my mother worked as a sales associate for Bloomingdale's, a famous department store, and was assigned to the children's department.

Some returning soldiers wanted their wives to stop working and stay home. It was too late. American women had proved they were smart, reliable, productive, and great at multi-tasking.

Then and Now

I've been a witness to history and seen the differences between yesterday's grandmas and today's grandmas.

My grandma never worked outside her home. To do so would have implied that her husband didn't earn enough money for his family. Finding care for five children would also have been a problem because day care centers didn't exist at the time. When I became a grandma, I had accrued a variety of work experience—a dozen years as a teacher, one summer as school secretary and phone operator (yes, I plugged in wires to connect callers), writer for a computer software firm, and freelance health/wellness writer. The difference in life experience between my grandmother and me in the role of grandmother is quite a contrast for such a relatively short period of time.

Yesterday's grandma made all meals from scratch. Today's grandma buys frozen meals, meal kits, take-out, or eats out.

Yesterday's grandma dried clothes on a clothesline and ironed them. Today's grandma uses a high-tech washer and dryer and asks, "What's an iron?"

Yesterday's grandma mended socks. Today's grandma buys socks when necessary and may even collect unusual socks.

Yesterday's grandma bought clothes from specialty shops— or made her own—and wore hats. Today's grandma orders clothes online and may wear a golf cap.

Yesterday's grandma cleaned rugs with a rug beater or vacuum. Today's grandma has a high-tech vacuum or robotic vacuum.

Yesterday's grandma walked so much she didn't need to think about exercise. Today's grandma belongs to a health club or uses a treadmill at home.

Yesterday's grandma relied on neighbors, church friends, and club members for social contacts. Today's grandma is on social media, Skype, and YouTube, posts on blogs, and sends photos from her smartphone.

Yesterday's grandma got her news from print media, radio, or newsreels. Today's grandma *is* the news, writing letters, supporting candidates, and running for office herself.

A huge shift has occurred during recent years.

> The grandma role changed from
> mentor to caregiver.

Why has this happened? Reasons include two-paycheck parents, death in the family (my story), and drug addiction. The opioid crisis has caused an increase in the number of grandparents raising grandchildren.[6] Children are being raised by both grandparents, or grandma alone, because grandparents are willing to fill a void and provide loving, stable homes for the next generation.

Caring for the Next Generation

Yesterday's grandmas didn't have many career options. Today's grandmas have so many career options it can be difficult to choose one. Many grandmas care for their grandchildren because both parents work.

A foodie friend of mine went to culinary school and became a trained chef. After she graduated, she was hired by a large organization in town. She loved her job and worked there until she was downsized (a terrible word). Disappointed as she was, my friend started to search for another chef job. Her search was short-lived because a new job appeared immediately— grandma. My friend agreed to care for her infant granddaughter five days a week. I didn't know this until I met her at the grocery store and saw an adorable baby sitting in the cart.

"Who's this?" I asked. My friend told me her story. I expected

---

6 "Number of Children Raised by Grandparents and Other Relatives Continues to Rise During Opioid Crisis," PR Newswire.

her to be bitter, but she was upbeat, happy, and devoted to her new role.

"I think I was meant to do this," she declared.

Grandparents fill many needed roles in the lives of families, Kelli Di Domenico writes in her article, "The Role of Grandparents in the Modern Family."[7] Spending time with grandkids can be a new beginning. For some grandmas, helping the family is a second chance. "Every child needs a hero," Di Dominico writes. "And who better to fill that role than their very own grandparent?" This role includes babysitter, historian, friend, teacher, and more.

> Contemporary grandmas have many
> talents and experiences to share.

When the twins were in first or second grade, Helen called before work to tell us the schools had closed due to blowing and drifting snow. She needed help and needed it fast. We jumped in the car and picked up the twins. On the way home, I wondered what I was going to do with them all day. Since I love to bake, I came up with the idea of making pizza from scratch. We made the dough and watched it rise, and the twins rolled it out with a pizza roller. The tool, which had one long roller and one short, seemed to fascinate them. They also liked putting pepperoni dots on the unbaked crust.

We put the pizza in the oven and waited impatiently for it to bake. Fifteen minutes later, the kitchen started to smell yeasty and spicy. The twins could hardly wait to taste the first bite of pizza. Lunch was a success because the twins helped make it. In the process, they learned about measuring, making yeast

---

7 Kelli Domanico, "The Role of Grandparents in the Modern Family," WPRI Eyewitness News.

dough, flattening dough, and pizza ingredients. After lunch the twins watched videos and played with toys from the toy cupboard. Ordinary experiences like making pizza can stay with grandkids for years.

Parenting expert Susan V. Bosak thinks the knowledge, skills, and ideas children pick up from grandparents stick with them more than those attained from other sources.[8] With the passage of time, an ordinary experience may become a special experience. Years later, your grandchild may recall the experience and repeat it with her or his children.

When my grandson was a teenager, he asked me to teach him to make French bread. I showed him how to pulse dough in the food processor, shape the dough into three long baguettes, slash the tops with a knife and set them on a perforated baguette pan. The pan was set on the top oven shelf, and I set a pan of ice cubes on the bottom. Steam from the melting cubes helped to crisp the loaves of bread. This experience must have influenced my grandson because he still likes to bake bread and loves to cook.

Sharing Generational Skills

You may not have realized how many talents you had until you became a grandma. Some talents are generational, passed down from one family to the next.

Your grandma may not have used recipes to prepare meals, for example. Instead, she used an informal measuring system she learned from her mother and grandmother: a pinch of this, an inch of that, butter the size of a walnut, a coffee cup of milk. Cooking instincts were involved too. Your grandma may have

8 Susan V. Bosak, "Why Grandparents are VIPs," Legacy Project.

known how to make jam, iron blouses and shirts, and maintain a vegetable garden.

Maybe you taught your granddaughter how to knit. Years from now, your granddaughter may knit a sweater for her child and think of you. A grandson may bake an apple pie using your recipe and eating the pie links him with you. The older I get, the more I realize that life's little moments, such as sitting around the table and drinking coffee with family members, are often big moments. I treasure the time I spent with my grandkids.

The twins have their own lives and I don't see them often, so when we're together I try to live mindfully. During recent visits they have been telling stories about us. "I remember the time you made wheat berry chili," my granddaughter said with a grimace. "It was awful." No doubt about it, the chili was awful, and I never made the recipe again. Still, I hope she remembers that I tried to prepare healthy, delicious meals—one of my goals as a grandma.

If your skills, such as playing the piano, have dwindled due to lack of practice, you could contact members of the extended family and ask them to share their skills with your grandchild. An uncle may be a woodworker and willing to demonstrate his tools and techniques, for example. This will make your grandchild aware of the talents and skills of family members. Years from now, your grandchild may recall the talents you shared and feel bolstered.

This chapter has contrasted the grandmothers of the past with grandmothers of the present. Today's grandmothers are no longer expected to knit and cook for their family—though they can if they want. Instead, today's grandmothers have career options and look for opportunities to share their talents and skills with their grandchildren. The next chapter tells how and why being a new grandma is a life-changing role. You may have experienced some changes already or are preparing for them. Preparation is helpful even for experienced grandmas. When you're prepared, you feel more confident. A confident grandma is an effective grandma.

CHAPTER 2

New Grandma, a Life-Changing Role

Writing a Mission Statement
What are You Called?
Some Life Changes
Wishes for Your Grandchild
Grandma Can Say No
Helping with Education
Joining a Support Group
Online Support

When you learned you were about to become a grandma, you were probably excited. Then you started asking questions about grandparenting. Answering those questions led to more questions. This chapter focuses on things new grandmas need to know, like what changes you can expect, how involved to get financially with your grandchild, where to find support, and choosing your grandma name. Even if you've been a grandma for a while, you may still pick up a few ideas on how to be the best grandma you can.

Writing a Mission Statement

Because I'm a writer, I know writing a book summary is helpful.

A book is off to a good start if writing the summary is easy. An easy summary means I've thought about the purpose, content, and audience of the book.

The summary idea may be applied to grandparenting. Instead of calling it a summary, I call it a mission statement. Think about your mission as a grandma and put it in writing. A one-sentence mission is best because it's easy to remember. When life gets confusing, go back and read your mission statement.

In theory, creating a one-sentence mission statement should only take a few hours. That didn't happen for me. Writing my mission statement took several days, and each revision was a reality check. Why was writing the statement hard? Later, when I thought about it, I realized that thoughts were crowding my mind. Minutes after a statement was on paper, I would have another idea to consider. Here's how my thinking went.

First mission statement: *I will be the best grandma ever.* Seconds later, I thought about the billions of talented grandmas in the world and the impossibility of leading the pack. This was a naïve, delusional superlative and needed to be adjusted. How does one know if she is the best grandma? What are the standards?

Second mission statement: *I will use my talents and education to be the best grandma I can be.* While this was an improvement, every grandma tries to be the best grandma she can, so the statement didn't feel very individual or special. To give my mind a rest, I stopped thinking about the mission statement for several days, and this proved to be a good decision.

Third mission statement: *Although I'm grieving, I will try to be a loving, supportive grandma.* This was a more realistic statement. After some thought, I decided to delete the word *grieving* because it was negative. I wanted my mission statement to be positive. *Loving* and *supportive* are positive words. Since I always try to do my best, I eliminated the word *try* from the statement.

Fourth and final mission statement: *I will use my talents and education to be a loving and supportive grandma.* Interestingly, this mission statement worked when John and I were raising the twins and works today because it applies to all ages and stages of human development.

> Writing a mission statement is
> a winnowing process.

Strong words, the ones with deep meaning and sound best, are kept. Other words, the weak and inappropriate ones, are discarded. This process can continue for days. I wrote for a while, rested for a while, wrote for a while, and so on. Figure out what works for you. You may wish to divide writing a mission statement into two parts: draft ideas and revision ideas. For many, including you, writing a mission statement may seem like a dated, old-fashioned idea, even a waste of time. Joanne Fritz, PhD, author and educator, would disagree with you strongly.[9]

Writing a mission statement is a modern idea that applies to people, businesses, and organizations, according to Fritz. She thinks the process of writing a statement focuses energy, clarifies purpose, and motivates you. Fritz, who has degrees in English and teaching, offers a very important tip for writing a mission statement: *Write short and only what you need.* I wished I had a neon sign of this statement above my computer. Since this wasn't possible, I printed out the advice and taped it to the

---

9 Joanne Fritz, "How to Write an Amazing Nonprofit Mission Statement," The Balance: Small Business.

top of the screen. For me and many other authors, writing short takes more time than writing long. Anyone can be wordy and go on and on without making a point. It takes time and effort to focus your ideas into a short, concise statement.

Although you may be tempted to write your mission statement mentally, not visually, please avoid this mistake because you will regret it later. Seeing a mission statement in writing makes it real. Printing the statement helps you to recall it when necessary. Write your draft ideas on paper or store them in a computer file. Words that seemed clear in your mind earlier can become blurry and hard to clarify when written down.

All of us have days when we wonder if we're doing things "right." Perhaps you have had some doubts. Negative self-talk can take you back to your mission statement. You may rethink the words you chose. It's a good idea to check your mission statement every few months. Are you still happy with it? Do you need to change a few words? The goal is to write a statement that passes the test of time.

Now you need to come up with a name. You can still be Marilyn or Susan or Yolanda, but you need a name that denotes your grandmother status.

What Are You Called?

New grandmas may grapple with this question. Choosing the "right" name involves self-image, personality, work experience, and life experience. I didn't want a sappy name, so I chose Grandma. Are you going to be Grandma, like me, or will you have a different name? I think a name should be something a grandchild can say from babyhood to adulthood. You may wish to test your name for a few weeks before you finalize it.

Worldwide, there are thousands of names for grandma and

many are related to language and culture. I chose the traditional *grandma* because it was easy and convenient. The twins always left out the letter D and called me Gramma. Because of this, I think of myself as Gramma.

Choosing a grandparent name can be almost as challenging as choosing a name for your child.[10] Some names are trendy and playful, whereas others are international, and based on culture. I've heard some grandkids call their grandmothers by their first names. To me, this seems overly familiar and a bit disrespectful. You can be a friendly grandma, but you aren't a sandbox friend, or soccer teammate, or high school classmate. Talk to your grandchild's parents about their kids calling you by your first name. How do they feel about it? Perhaps they have some suggestions for names. Like many grandmas, your name may turn out to be a mispronunciation, such as Wamma for grandma, or one that represents your personality, such as Funny Girl.

Some Life Changes

Change is a constant of life, and becoming a grandma is no exception. Both new and experienced members of the Grandma Force need to stay aware of changes. For one thing, your identity has probably expanded. In your teenage years you babysat for 50 cents an hour. Now you may be babysitting for free. Frequent flyers miles are adding up because you visit your grandkids so often. Your grandchild may spend two glorious summer weeks with you. Perhaps you accompanied your grandchild on her or his college search to provide support. Some life changes are welcome and others, not so welcome.

10 Bethany Kandel, "How to Choose Your Grandparent Name: Sometimes You Pick Your Name. Sometimes It Picks You," Grandparents.com.

Lack of quiet time was one change I experienced. I need quiet time for research and to write, but had little quiet time, down time, and was always on the go. Although the twins were fifteen years old and could do much for themselves, keeping up with their schedules was tiring. Grieving for four family members was tiring too. When I went to bed at night I was exhausted. Some life changes were challenging, but I accepted them, and looked upon these changes as expressions of love. I wanted the twins to be happy again.

Becoming a grandparent may intersect with other life transitions[11]—not the best timing. You may become a grandparent at the same time as you receive a job promotion. You may become a grandparent just as you return to college. I became a grandparent when my writing career was starting to take off. Sometimes I felt torn between spending time on writing and spending time on grandparenting. I felt this way again when the twins moved in with us. My solution was to get up an hour earlier, write for an hour, and then fix breakfast for the twins.

The degree of closeness between grandma and grandchild is influenced by affection, association, family, family obligations, geographic proximity, and helping behavior. How close you feel to your grandchild also depends on the things you do together. An AARP survey[12] ranked the top six activities: eating together, watching television, computer games, overnights, shopping for clothes, and exercise/sports. What activities do you and your grandchild like to do together?

---

11 Bosak, "Grandparents Today," The Legacy Project.
12 Bosak, "Grandparents Today," The Legacy Project.

Wishes for Your Grandchild

All grandmas have similar wishes for their grandkids.

We want them to be healthy, happy, get an education, use their talents, and follow their dreams. But your dream for a grandchild may not be their dream. Maybe you're musical and want your grandchild to take piano lessons. However, your grandchild may prefer sports. Within seconds, the dream of a grandchild giving piano concerts for community groups is dashed.

Every grandchild has the right to dream. Just make sure you support your grandchild's dreams, not your dreams.

Think of some of the wishes you have for your grandchild, wishes that enable her or him to choose their own path. One grandma may wish her grandchild to have the career she wanted. Another grandma may wish peace, love, happiness, and a sense of self for her granddaughter. Yet another grandma may want her grandchildren to find true love and faith.

Wishing is fun, but you need to be realistic. Chances are a non-athletic grandchild isn't going to be the star of the football team.

Brainstorm on ways to help your grandchild achieve their wishes. For example, you may buy a lightweight bat and softball for your grandson. Before you know it, you're cheering at Little League games. Giving a grandchild books about her or his hobby is another idea. Reading changes lives, and I've always believed kids can have too many toys and never too many books. You may buy a small book shelf or bookends for your grandchild's collection.

When John and I were raising the twins, we became involved

in high school activities again in order to support their interests. We cheered for our granddaughter at gymnastics meets
and cheered for our grandson at band concerts. We drove to St.
Paul to enter our granddaughter's photos in a Minnesota State
Fair contest and she won a blue ribbon—one of her dreams.

Even if you think you're doing a good job, some improvement
may be needed. Jeanne Segal, PhD, and Lawrence Robinson offer
suggestions in their article, "How to Be a Better Grandparent."[13]
Segal and Robinson think the best grandparenting activities
flow naturally from grandparents' and grandchildren's
interests. For the flow to happen, you need to be available to
your grandchild. Perhaps you have a favorite activity that you
enjoy, such as going to car shows or biking on city trails.

Taking it easy together is another suggestion, or as folks in
my generation said, "Sit down and take a load off."

If you feel stressed, you have the mental power to switch
gears and slow down. Slowing down helps your grandchild to
slow down and appreciate the time you spend together. One-
on-one time together is another suggestion. Occasionally my
grandson or granddaughter would have one-on-one time with
me. While these times were special, they didn't happen often.
Twins come in pairs, and most of my time was spent with both
of my grandchildren.

Think about the kinds of activities you and your grandchild
could enjoy together. Would these activities be beneficial?
Does your grandchild do well in a group or prefer individual
attention? Take advantage of the events in your community.
Concerts, plays, movies, museums, and walks give you time
to exchange ideas with your grandchild. Public libraries have
many free speakers and activities for the public.

---

13 Jeannae Segal and Lawrence Robinson, "How to Be a Better Grandparent," Help Guide.

Grandma Can Say No

One of the most important things you need to know as a new grandma is that you can say no. This may seem like common sense, but I think saying no is especially difficult for new grandmas.

> Being a grandma doesn't mean
> you say yes to everything.

A friend of mine is a devoted grandmother. Her daughter and son-in-law both worked, so she said yes to every caregiving request. The grandkids came for overnights and weekends. She cared for her grandkids when they were sick. One would think this was enough, but this grandma also planned special activities for her grandkids. Life was good until my friend developed a chronic illness. Several years passed and, during this time, my friend became pale, tired, and wan.

"You've got to say no or you're going to wear yourself out," another friend advised.

"I can't," my friend replied. "The family needs me."

This conversation was repeated time and again. Although my friend continued to care for her grandchildren, she complained of exhaustion. Finally, she was too exhausted to care for them and forced to say no.

You may have already learned this lesson. "No" is a protective response. Although you said no to extra babysitting, you may have said yes to having a grandchild come for the weekend. You may say yes to taking your grandchild to the zoo or children's museum. Add as many yes responses to your life as you feel comfortable with. But if you feel you need to say no, do it. You will feel better. Standing up for yourself is a right and normal. Saying no doesn't diminish your power as a member of the Grandma Force, and in fact gives you the stamina and courage to make other healthy choices for yourself.

Helping with Education

As a new grandma, you find yourself thinking about the future. You picture your grandchild going off to school, finishing high school, and leaving for college or trade school. Now may be the time to think about helping your grandchild with college costs—a big commitment. Many options exist, and your challenge is to find the option that works best. Regardless of what you decide, make sure to keep track of how much you gift to your grandchild for budgeting purposes.

Grandparents control 75 percent of the nation's wealth.[14] Much of this cash outlay goes to grandkids. A MetLife survey stated grandparents spend an average of $1,700 per year on their grandkids.[15]

One common way that grandparents support grandchildren is by contributing to their college fund. Some grandparents give grandkids money for college at holiday time. This gift has the potential to make a huge impact in a grandchild's life. Crunch the numbers. Starting with infancy, if you give your grandchild $200 each holiday, by the time they are eighteen years old, she or he will have $3,600. Throw in birthday money and the total is higher. Add money your grandchild earns, and the total is higher still. Getting money for college isn't an exciting gift, so

---

14 Jeff Anderson, "Why Grandparents Matter More Than Ever," Senior Living Blog.
15 Anderson, "Why Grandparents Matter More Than Ever," Senior Living Blog.

you may want to temper it with a small gift to open, such as a coffee mug or school sweatshirt.

Another option is to start a 529 education savings plan for your grandchild. This US government plan is designed to encourage saving for college and usually has better interest rates than a normal savings or checking account.[16] Helping to pay for a grandchild's college education is a way to assure a bright future. Even if you only put a small amount in the fund, the fact that you are doing it may motivate your grandchild. You are acting as a financial role model.

Financial writer Kathryn Flynn writes that sending tuition payments directly to the college or university may be the best choice, and it's easy to do.[17] The twins' college costs were paid out of their mother's estate, and they were grateful for her foresight. We've been impressed with the twins' money management. Although I know nothing about their current financial situations, I think they used some of their inheritance for emergencies and education.

Other options include loaning money to a grandchild, setting up an education trust fund, putting money into a custodial account, paying off a grandchild's student loans, and putting money into a savings account. It's wise to consult a financial planner about these options. You may have to consult a lawyer as well. For example, when loaning a grandchild money, you will need to determine how and when you are paid back. Consult a financial advisor about a realistic payment schedule and a lawyer about federal and state tax laws.

Worthy as these ideas are, you may not be able to contribute in significant financial ways to your grandchild's education.

---

16 "How Grandparents Can Help Fund College," Fidelity.
17 Kathryn Flynn, "10 Easy Ways Grandparents Can Help Pay for College," Saving for College.

Don't feel guilty. There are other ways to help, such as talking about the values of education as your grandchild grows. "A college education changes you," I told my daughters. "Once you have it, nobody can take it from you." My younger daughter has repeated this quote many times.

If your grandchild has shown interest in fitness and bicycling, you may give her or him a subscription to a bicycling magazine. Books on the topic may also be welcome. You may do an Internet search of the topic, print out articles, stick them in page protectors, and put the pages in a three-ring binder. This gift may help your grandchild plan her or his future.

Joining a Support Group

Joining a grandma support group is a proactive decision for a new grandma. I think the grandmas of the world need to be connected and support each other. Joining a support group is one way to do this. If you find talking over the back fence doesn't provide adequate connection and support for you in your grandma journey, a grandma support group might be a good decision.

Before you join a support group you need to know how it works. A support group brings together people who are facing similar issues.[18] A support group isn't a replacement for licensed medical care or counseling. Peers may form a support group for a specific purpose. The local hospital may have support groups on specific health issues, such as diabetes. High schools may have support groups for grieving students, including the loss of a pet. A support group may also function as an open forum for discussion. Joining a support group makes you feel less lonely

---

18 "Support Groups: Make Connections, Get Help," Mayo Clinic.

and isolated. Over time, you may start to feel empowered. Group meetings give you chances to express your feelings. Members will have many tips for interacting with grandkids.

How do you find a group? Your healthcare provider may be able to provide leads. The Department of Social Services may have information on groups for grandmothers. Search on the Internet for grandma or grandparent support groups in your area.

When you've found one or a few that seem like they would work for you, "test drive" a few meetings, and see if they are beneficial. At the first few meetings, you may choose to listen and not contribute. When you feel comfortable, you may share your thoughts. Learn about the group facilitator. Does she or he have special training or extensive experience? Talk with a group member if possible and ask if they are benefiting from the group. Find out how often the group meets. Everyone should get a chance to talk. One person can dominate the group unless the facilitator intervenes. A support group is for everyone and everyone should have a chance to speak. Some support groups have activities for members.

> You don't have to be friends with everyone
> in the group to benefit from meetings.

I started a support group some years ago and it was a learning experience. Although the group was small, members had the same goal—to have a safe place to share experiences and feelings. A local church let us meet in a lower level room free of charge. To publicize the group, I wrote a brochure and contacted the local newspaper. The newspaper printed a notice about the group on its community page. We met once a week. At the beginning of every meeting, I reminded the members about confidentiality. "What's said in group stays in group." Unfortunately, sometimes a support group turns into a gripe group, and if this happens, you have the right to leave.[19]

I also belong to The Compassionate Friends, an international organization for those who have suffered the loss of a child. Local chapter members go out to dinner once a month.

Support groups can be ultra-specialized, such as a group for Native American women in Abita Springs, Louisiana.[20] The group is based on the prophecy, "When the grandmothers speak, the Earth will heal." The women gather together to heal the earth and leave with a sense of peace and sisterhood. Women ages fifty and beyond are welcome. Although members call themselves grandmothers, they may not have biological children. Group meetings include smudging with sage, an opening exercise, selected reading, passing the talking bowl, drumming, and singing. Donations are welcome although there are no group fees.

I love the idea of grandmothers healing the earth. I love the idea of grandmothers joining together to help grandchildren. I love the idea of creating meaningful lives together. As you consider what your role as grandma looks like, you may realize that you need some help.

Online Support

Most contemporary grandmas are wired. They know how to use a smart phone, computer, and the Internet. Grandmas turn to the Internet for information and support. I used the search words *websites for grandmas* and was boggled by the number of listings that appeared. Many websites were for grandmas and

19 "Support Groups: Make Connections, Get Help," Mayo Clinic.
20 "Grandmother Group," Women's Center for Healing.

grandpas, but there were few for grandmas only. Don't waste your time on vapid, disorganized, or pushy websites. When you log into a website the question to answer is,

"Does this website really help me?"

The following websites help in a variety of ways: blog posts, question and answer columns, recipes, and more. My comments are based on website design, ease of use, and the feelings I felt.

www.grandmasbriefs.com This is a blog written by Lisa Carpenter, a freelance writer and former newspaper editor. She started the blog in 2009 after she couldn't find current information for grandmas like herself. The first visual you see is underpants on a clothesline, a photo that gets your attention. Carpenter's blog tabs include Recipes, Puzzles, Brag Book, Spotlight (for special grandmas), and Back Room (product reviews). To me, Back Room is a confusing title, but I like the variety that Carpenter's blog offers.

www.gagasisterhood.com Donne Davis founded the social network in 2003. It has a broad mission: 1) explore modern grandparenting; 2) share wisdom; 3) inspire other grandmas. The GaGa Sisterhood is a national network with local chapters. Chapter news and book recommendations are available on the website. "Ask GaGa" is a helpful feature and your questions will be answered by Donne Davis herself. I used a GaGa Sisterhood article for this book.

www.coolgrandma.com This website describes itself as a "comprehensive destination" and it certainly seems to be that. Instead of tabs, the online community has you click on headings for information. The headings include Today's Featured Articles, Learning Center, Chat Rooms, eCards, Tutorials, and more. You will find a wealth of information under each heading. When I clicked on some headings, I received error signals. With an update, this website could really deliver.

www.grandmaideas.com As the name implies, this website offers ideas for grandmothers to do with grandkids. It uses a click-to-read-more approach. When you click on an article, more articles appear. Topics include real-life stuff such as "Party in Your PJs." The articles are practical and graphics below the main headings lead to additional information.

www.grandmother-blog.com/blog This website is written by a PhD baby boomer who calls herself Mema. Tab choices include grandparenting basics, including gifts for grandkids, meals/recipes, and family travel. As Mema writes, "Sharing the joy of grandparenting is also a chronicle of the discovery of the miracle of grandparenting—pure and innocent mutual unconditional love and adoration." I like Mema's philosophy and share it.

www.gransnet.com According to the website, this is a social network for those fifty years and older in the United Kingdom. Most of the categories seem to be aimed at women. The categories: forums, books, competitions that offer prizes, food (recipes including fruitcake), style and beauty, legal, and money. The one tab that's missing is the About tab, so you don't know who owns or manages the website or its physical address. I could spend hours on this site.

www.aarp.org Although this website isn't just for grandmas, I include it here because AARP has made grandparents, especially grandparents raising grandkids (GRGs), a top priority. For example, if you click on the "Relationships" heading, you will find an article about grandparent rights. Many other timely articles are available from this site. You can also find helpful articles in the AARP magazine and newsletter.

www.grandparentsraisinggrandchildrenworldwide.com
Ten percent of all the grandparents in America are raising their grandchildren, according to the US Census Bureau, and this number is going up. This website tells real, heartbreaking stories about grandparents who are raising their grandchildren due to addicted parents. Looking for legal advice and counsel is one theme. You'll find useful tips too, such as how to get a grandchild to eat vegetables. Photos of happy grandchildren balance the sad grandparenting stories. This is a real, reliable site and I recommend it to GRGs.

I am blessed to be a grandma in the computer age. Technology links me to other grandmas, websites, and resources. This chapter discussed some of the things a new grandma needs to know and do. The next chapter tells you how to settle into the grandmother role and plan a future with your grandchild. I compare this experience to writing a script. You are the author of your script and, with input from your grandchild and parents, can plan memorable family events that add up to an exciting plot.

CHAPTER 3

Writing Your Grandma Script

Each grandparent-grandchild relationship
is special in its own way.

As you get to know your grandchild, and your grandchild gets to know you, a new script emerges. That's exciting. Even more exciting, you can write the script and determine some of the scenes. A new relationship is developing right before your eyes, something journalist Lesley Stahl discovered.[21] Stahl describes herself as a tough journalist, yet her toughness disappeared instantly when she held her granddaughter for the first time. "I was jolted, blindsided by a wallop of loving more intense than anything I could remember," she writes.

---

21 Stahl, Leslie, "On Becoming a Grandmother," AARP.

Script Components

Although you can't predict how the grandma-grandchild relationship will develop, you have some influence over it. You can spend time with your grandchild, foster her or his interests, be an attentive listener, and explore your feelings. Becoming a grandma generates new feelings. At least, that's my experience. Previously, I mentioned that becoming a grandma happened when my career was just taking off. It wasn't the best timing. As my script evolved, however, I found new things to write about, including caregiving and grandparenting.

A close relationship between generations strengthens the family. Sharing your wisdom and knowledge helps your grandchild. She or he may learn organizational skills from you or develop a new passion, such as golf. When your grandchild reaches adulthood, your influence will be remembered.

When I was grieving for four family members, I thought about my immigrant grandparents—German on my father's side, British on my mother's side—and the courage they showed when they came to America. Both sets of grandparents came from working families and this work ethic served them well in their new land. I was comforted by the previous generation's example. Their genes were part of me and if they were courageous, I could be courageous and survive multiple losses.

You have the ingredients for your script: family history, present family, work experience (including running a household), innate talent, learned skills, education, and determination. Think of what your script could include and focus on things that are meaningful to you and your grandchild.

Grandparenting expert Linda Eyre, author of *Grandmoth-*

ering, thinks it's important to ask questions.[22] Ask your grandchild about their favorite things, what scares them, what worries them, and what they would like to become. These types of questions help you understand the uniqueness of each grandchild. Asking questions was so important to Eyre that she and her husband sent questionnaires to their grandchildren before a family reunion. One grandchild wrote, "I will never ride a bike naked in public!" The grandchild had seen this and didn't want to repeat the scene. Eyre thinks questions can spark storytelling, which is part of family history.

Personal Goals

Personal goals are part of your script. As your grandchild grows, she or he will have their goals, and you will have yours. These goals can be woven into your narrative. Asking yourself questions helps you clarify personal goals. New grandmas and experienced ones may have different goals. Think about your goals and whether they are realistic. What goal is more important to you? Goals can change with time, as I discovered.

One of my first goals was to teach the twins how to say "grandma" and "grandpa." As the twins grew up and changed, so did my goals. One goal I had was to attend my granddaughter's gymnastic meets. I hadn't attended gymnastics meets before and felt like I was the oldest woman there. A toddler approached me, pointed her finger, and announced, "You grandma." She did this at every meet. Yes, I was a grandma—a grandma supporting her granddaughter—and I attended all the gymnastic meets. The meets were fun, helped me learn more about my granddaughter, and gymnastics in

22 Linda Eyre. *Grandmothering: The Secrets to Making a Difference While Having the Time of Your Life* (Sanger, CA: Familius, 2018), 62-66.

general. Two established goals, maintaining a writing career and volunteering in the community, remained in my script.

The failure to reach a goal can be beneficial,

as this story about my French lessons illustrates. I took two years of French in high school. When I reached middle age, I started dreaming about French vocabulary words night after night. *Oeuf*, the word for egg, is one word I dreamed about. So many French words surfaced from my subconscious I decided to take French lessons from a friend. To say my friend was fluent in French would be an understatement. She lived, walked, and talked French, including slang, and had been to France many times. Her husband took French lessons from her too.

My goal was to be able to carry on a basic conversation. When my friend learned John and I were going to an international conference in Paris, she gave me a "cheat sheet" of common words and sentences. The list came in handy and my limited French worked. I managed to order a very specific dinner in a neighborhood restaurant. When we wanted more wine, I ordered two glasses, one *rouge* and one *blanc*. To balance our order of steak, I ordered green beans, or *haricot verts*.

John was impressed and a little worried. "We're okay if you always order the same menu," he commented. "If we want anything else, we're in trouble."

"*Oui*," I answered, trying to sound French.

We stayed in a charming hotel near the conference center. The hotel had a small antique elevator with a perforated, retractable door (a bit scary), and comfortable rooms. Breakfast was included. One morning, I impulsively ordered a boiled egg for breakfast and it cost eight dollars. That's a lot of money for an egg in any language. But I was in Paris, in a breakfast room that looked like a drawing from a children's picture book, with the man I loved dearly. What better place to eat a pricey egg? The egg arrived in an old-fashioned egg cup and I enjoyed it. I didn't order another egg, however. One *oeuf* was enough.

Shortly after we returned home, family responsibilities started to interfere with French lessons and they slowly waned. I didn't reach my goal of becoming conversant in French. Nevertheless, the lessons were beneficial. I had challenged myself, identified the action steps (find a teacher and find the time), activated old study habits, and did my homework faithfully. The most important thing I learned was that I could still learn, and this was encouraging.

It's important to set goals both for your interactions with your grandchild—like attending all gymnastics meets—and for yourself and your personal improvement. On your way to personal improvement, look out for the perfectionist trap.

Avoiding the Perfectionist Trap

Trying to be a good grandma is normal. The quest for perfection can become abnormal. You can improve your grandchild's future by avoiding the perfectionist trap. This is the kind of trap that can sneak up on you. Birthday parties for a grandchild are an example. When planning a birthday party becomes more about the production of the party—live animals or a hired magician, you may be trying for perfection.

Perfectionism is a fast and enduring track to unhappiness. Every day, perhaps every hour, the perfectionist works on her endless report card and tries to avoid failure.[23] But the perfectionist is chasing a moving target.

---

23 Monica Ramirez Basco, "The Perfect Trap," Psychology Today.

The failure to reach the perfection target leads to procrastination. If you never reach your goal, why bother to do anything? The fear of failure causes the perfectionist to delay action. Before long, occasional procrastination becomes a habit. Repeated failure can lead to depression. The perfectionist may unknowingly distance herself from others.

Thankfully, you can break free of perfectionism. If you're headed for it, put on the brakes now by doing the following: Give yourself credit for what you accomplish. Talk to others—family members, church friends, close friends—and ask if they think you've fallen into the perfectionist trap. Make changes when necessary.

Progress is the goal, not perfection.

You don't need to wear yourself out to be a good grandma. Having a dominant trait doesn't mean you're a perfectionist. Because I like neatness, some people think I'm a perfectionist. "You are very particular," one of John's caregivers commented. Her delivery made it sound like she thought I was a perfectionist. The truth of the matter is that messes distract me and make me uncomfortable, reactions that come from childhood.

We lived in a small tract house. My father was a salesman and needed a home office. Since the basement was packed with stuff, he used the dining room as his office. Half the dining room table was covered with files. Before we ate a meal, we had to shift folders aside. Additional folders lined the perimeter of the dining room. More papers were on the kitchen table and on the floor of my parents' bedroom.

The migrating folders drove me nuts. I think they drove my mother nuts, but she never said a word. Folders represented accounts, accounts represented income, and income represented security. Every so often, Dad would cull his files, and the house would look neat. But a few days later, more files appeared. Living with clutter was torture for an artistic person like me. In defense, I turned my bedroom into a haven. Before I left for school, I made the bed, hung up my clothes, and stashed homework in desk drawers.

Mom was so impressed with my tidy room she showed it to her sister. I found them peering in the doorway of my room as if they had made an archeological discovery. "Isn't that something," my aunt declared, and Mom nodded her head in agreement. Their "something" was my survival. Neatness is still important to me, and I tidy our home daily. Most importantly, I know the difference between neatness and perfectionism. Examine what's important to you and determine if you're pursuing those goals with a healthy motivation for improvement or an unhealthy perfectionist attitude.

Grandkids aren't expecting perfectionism from us. They want love, support, and understanding. You can be that grandma. Being a loving grandma can make you seem perfect to your grandchild. In time, you may become your grandchild's role model, something you never expected.

I'm a Role Model!

Whether you like it or not, you are modeling behavior for your grandchild. While you're going about your business, your grandchild is gathering clues about your personality, problem-solving skills, sense of humor (or lack of it), adaptability, and coping skills. In many ways, your grandchild is your understudy. You aren't just a grandma, you're a caregiver, mentor, leader, mediator, negotiator, humorist, historian, and family representative.

According to Marilyn Price-Mitchell, PhD, five qualities matter in a good role model: the ability to inspire, a clear set of values, commitment to community, selflessness, and the ability to overcome obstacles.[24] In response to a comment on her article, Price-Mitchell wrote, "Often, we need to see qualities in others before we realize those same qualities are in us." Consider the role models in your life. Did they demonstrate those five qualities? Do you?

By the time children are adolescents, they can tell the difference between positive and negative behaviors, including the behaviors of people they admire. Sadly, some children don't have good role models. They may even have harmful ones.

Jerry Schreur and Judy Schreur, authors of *Creative Grandparenting*, discuss modeling in "Grandparents as Role Models."[25] Sometimes parents aren't worthy role models, and kids turn to grandparents for guidance. Using verses from the Bible as support, the Schreurs say grandparents can model morals, gender, values, and godly behavior. Talking about values is different from living them. Though a grandchild may or may not listen to your words, she or he will always remember your actions.

> A grandma's actions speak louder
> than her words.

John and I hoped the twins saw us as positive role models. When the twins lived with us John and I tried to model mutual respect. I wondered if the twins noticed this and decided to

---

24 Marilyn Price-Mitchell, "What is a Role Model? Five Qualities that Matter to Youth," Roots of Action.
25 Jerry Schreur and Judy Schreur, "Grandparents as Role Models," Focus on the Family.

email them about it. My email read, "I'm working on a new book, *The Grandma Force*, and am writing about being a role model. Grandpa and I tried to model respectful behavior when you lived with us. Not only do we love each other, we respect each other. Did you pick up on our mutual respect? If so, what were the clues?"

My granddaughter thought our conversations showed mutual respect and suspected some conversations were held in private. "We didn't see you fight or disagree, and I believe all of these conversations happened, but not in front of others. You both respected the different roles you had and how you each uniquely contributed to the household."

In my grandson's reply, he said my question was a doozy. The next sentence made me cry. "You and grandpa have helped shape me into the person I am today in so many ways." He went on to say that I was an example of how thoughtful exploration of loss and tragedy can lead to renewed purpose and becoming a resource for others. "Your resilience has always impressed me and it is something I strive to follow," he wrote.

In a later conversation, my grandson said he noticed that John and I didn't fight. We rarely disagree and, when we do, it is in a low key, respectful way. We never call each other names or yell at each other or make accusations. In sixty-one years of marriage, we've never had a fight.

I think the lack of fighting comes in part from our similar approach to money management, a source of contention for many couples. I describe myself as Mrs. Pinch Penny and John appreciates my careful approach. If I say we need something, the need is probably real. If I say something needs to be repaired, the need is real, and we call a repair person. "I never worry about you and money," John has said many times.

Respect is perhaps the most important quality we can role

model for our grandchildren. Whether it's husband and wife, parent and child, grandparent and grandchild, mutual respect is essential for a relationship to work. Love without respect is dangerous and can crush another person. To foster respect, we need to understand others, learn how to mesh personal needs with theirs, and help the other person achieve what they want. This means we learn to treat each other as we would like to be treated.[26]

You can model respect every time you're with your grandchild. Respect will be evident at family gatherings, social gatherings, and with strangers. Modeling good behavior helps your grandchild determine personal behavior. They may think, "I can be kind to animals like Grandma," or "When she talks to people, Grandma never yells." Perhaps most importantly, remember to respect yourself as a grandma.

Ditching Grandma Guilt

Lisa Carpenter writes about grandma guilt trips in an American Grandparents website article.[27] Her list of guilt triggers includes saying no, saying yes, negative thoughts, not being an activity director, not visiting enough, and not buying enough. Let's explore these triggers further.

Sarah Zadok, a childbirth educator and doula (a birth companion/coach), responded to one grandma who felt guilt for saying no.[28] This grandma said she hoped to take some classes and participate more at synagogue, ideas that upset her

26 Peter Gray, "In Relationships, Respect May Be Even More Crucial than Love," Psychology Today.
27 Lisa Carpenter, "Top 6 Grandparent Guilt Trips—And How to Overcome Them," Grandparents.com.
28 Sarah Zadok, "Grandmother = Free Babysitter," The Jewish Woman.

daughter. The daughter expected her mother to watch her baby while she was at work. The writer didn't know what to do and signed her letter, "Torn Grandma."

Zadok's answer pointed out some important truths. A grandma who is constantly giving can become exhausted and depleted. Putting yourself first doesn't mean you're neglecting the family. The opposite is true, and if you're making yourself a better person, this benefits the family. Finally, a grandma needs to nourish her soul by studying and praying each day. This advice comes from the Jewish tradition, yet religion and spirituality are important to many grandmas.

How you nourish your soul is less important than doing it. Whether it's prayer, a walk, or a nap, figure out what nourishes you. You'll find more information about spirituality and religion in Chapter 12, "Taking Care of Me."

Author Barbara Graham had a problem saying yes.[29] She writes about how she enjoyed being with her grandkids, yet she felt slightly underappreciated and like a powerless servant. Because she always said yes, her grown children had a sense of entitlement, and that can make a loving grandma work harder. Graham admits to being so tired her vision gets blurry and she gets "a tad cranky." Her experience points out the need for members of the Grandma Force to set limits. Not babysitting may be one of them.

I felt guilty from negative thoughts that surfaced when I compared my grandparenting to my sister-in-law's grand-parenting. My sister-in-law knit sweaters for her grandkids, knit toys for them, and made gingerbread houses with them at Christmas time. Making gingerbread houses became a family tradition. I didn't do any of these things. Then I thought about

---

29 Barbara Graham, "We All Want to Help with the Kids, but No One Wants to be Taken for Granted," AARP.

the things I had done. I made salt dough for sculptures, went for walks with the twins, put on puppet shows, took them to museums, and wrote a song for them.

The twins were three years old, interested in crawly creatures, and aware of humor. They loved the funny last line of my song.

> Buggy, buggy bugs in buggy, buggy rugs,
> Singing a buggy song,
> Buggy, buggy bugs in buggy, buggy rugs,
> Singing all day long.
> Buggy, buggy bugs in buggy, buggy rugs,
> Doing a buggy dance.
> I'd rather have bugs in buggy, buggy rugs,
> Than buggies in my pants!

Contemporary grandmas may feel that being an activity director is how grandmas are supposed to act, and the time they spend with their grandkids becomes over-scheduled. I made this mistake. Helen and the twins were joining us for a weekend at the family cabin. In preparation for the weekend, I bought a sun print kit and some games. Like blueprint paper, sun print, or cyanotype paper, creates white images on a blue background. Leaves, flowers, and grasses are laid on the paper and set out in the sun to develop the pictures. While Helen appreciated my thoughtfulness and planning, she had a different take on it.

"I want the kids to learn how to entertain themselves," she explained. She didn't press the point, so I didn't feel guilty about providing the supplies, but I did learn from the experience.

Not being able to visit grandkids can be a source of guilt. Today, it's common for generations to live thousands of miles apart. Some grandmas and grandkids live on opposite coasts.

You can't afford to fly from New York City to San Francisco every month. Even if you live in the same town as your grandkids, work responsibilities or illness may prevent you from seeing them. This makes you sad and increases guilt feelings.

The final guilt source Carpenter cites is not buying enough.[30] School costs keep going up and many grandmas pay for paper, pencils, markers, calculators, backpacks, and fees. Perhaps your grandchild expects generous birthday or Christmas gifts. While this help is welcome, you know you can't give your grandchildren as much as they want and still pay your bills. You need to work out a solution to your dilemma, and the fact that you must do this adds to your guilt.

Ongoing guilt is harmful to your health and wellbeing. Like a character in Shakespeare's play, *Macbeth*, you may want to shout, "Out, damn guilt, out!" Thank goodness there are ways to get rid of guilt. One of Carpenter's suggestion is to adapt the AA Serenity Prayer to your situation: accept what you can't change, change the things you can, and have the wisdom to know the difference. Another wise thing to do is figure out what type of grandma you are or plan to be.

Now you know about the components of your personal grandma script that tells the story of your grandma-grandchild relationship. These components include learning from setbacks, ditching guilt, being a role model, avoiding perfectionism, and the importance of new goals. More importantly, each part adds up to an exciting life, and it's yours. You are sharing your life with a beloved grandchild. The next chapter describes different types of grandmothers. Which type will you turn out to be?

---

30 Lisa Carpenter, "Top 6 Grandparent Guilt Trips—And How to Overcome Them," Grandparents.com.

CHAPTER 4

Types of Grandmas

Formal Grandma
Fun-Seeking Grandma
Grandma Raising Grandkids
Wise Grandma
Long-Distance Grandma
Working Grandma
The Nanny Granny
Other Types of Grandmas

Just like there are a million kinds of people, so there are a million kinds of grandmas. This chapter discusses some of the types. Susan Krauss Whitbourne, PhD, professor of psychology at the University of Massachusetts in Amherst, gives us five types[31]—formal grandma, fun-seeking grandma, grandma raising grandkids, wise grandma, and long-distance grandma. I added two more types, the working grandma and the nanny granny. As you read the descriptions, see what parts fit the role of grandma you are creating for yourself. Keep in mind you may be a combination of characteristics from different types of grandmas. Few grandmas fit only one type.

---

31 Susan Krauss Whitbourne, "Five Types of Grandparents and How They Shape Your Lives," *Psychology Today.*

Formal Grandma

This grandma follows the guidelines that she thinks are appropriate and necessary in society. Her guidelines include good manners, proper clothing, modesty, courtesy, and conversation skills. A formal grandma may not be overly involved in childcare, according to Whitbourne. As American society has become more casual, I've seen only a few formal grandmas in my life, and one was my mother-in-law.

Nana was a *very* formal grandma. Although she was a trained nursery school teacher and loved children, she seemed to appreciate children more when they were infants, toddlers, and nursery schoolers. Nana's interest in her grandchildren waned as the kids grew older. When we asked Nana to become more involved with our daughters, her reply was, "I'm a Victorian grandmother," whatever that meant. I think being with older grandchildren made her nervous.

Surprisingly, Nana and Pampa agreed to take care of our daughters when we went to a conference in Europe. We were gone for two weeks. Years later, we learned Nana recruited many other relatives to care for the girls. Family members we barely knew took them in. No matter how much she loved her grandchildren, two weeks were too much for Nana, the Victorian grandmother.

Manners were important to Nana. At dinner time, no elbows were allowed on the table. Using a toothpick at the table was frowned upon. Blowing your nose at the table was a no-no. Nana was shocked when a local dignitary visited her home, sat down on the couch, and casually plopped his feet on the coffee table. She talked about his mistake for weeks, and even commented on the size of his feet. "What a thing to do!" she exclaimed. "He is an educated man and should know better."

Formal grandmas are so focused on proper behavior that they correct their grandchildren constantly. Nobody, not even a member of the Grandma Force, wants to be corrected constantly. Such reproofs, especially in public, put a damper on self-confidence. If your grandchild exhibits a behavior that you find problematic, consider talking to their parents, or talking to them one-on-one later. Postponing a discussion gives you time to choose your points and practice them.

Fun-Seeking Grandma

The fun-seeking grandma focuses on leisure and entertainment. She is always thinking of amazing things to do with her grandkids, planning the activities, and coordinating them. Grandkids may think of the fun-seeking grandma as a tour guide, and this may be her main role. The fun-seeking grandma may be the ever-smiling grandma. Watching a fun-seeking grandma in action can be tiring because she has so much energy.

Linda Eyre, mother of nine and grandmother of thirty-two, is a fun-seeking grandma.[32] When she and her husband planned family reunions, their goal was to provide exciting, memorable times for their grandchildren. Eyre shares tips for planning family reunions in her book, *Grandmothering*. Her book includes sample planning documents and recipes for feeding a crowd. Other grandmas can learn something from the fun-seeking grandma, starting with enthusiasm.

It's more fun to be with an upbeat grandma than a complainer. I asked one of our paid caregivers what her grandma was like and she smiled. "My grandma went from being a hippie to becoming an engineer." The caregiver recalled the time she

32 Linda Eyre, *Grandmothering: The Secrets to Making a Difference While Having the Time of Your Life* (Sanger, California: Familius, 2018).

visited a fountain water park with her grandma. "She was in her sixties at the time, put on her bathing suit, and splashed in the fountains with me." I bet her grandma was fun!

While I'm not the fun-seeking grandma, I did plan fun things to do with my grandkids, laughed a lot, and had fun with them. Chapter 8, "At-Home Activities for Grandkids," and Chapter 9, "Out-and-About Activities for Grandkids," contain a wealth of information about having fun with your grandkids.

Grandmas Raising Grandkids (GRG)

Whitbourne refers to this grandma type as a *surrogate parent*.[33] Grandmas who are raising their grandkids aren't replacements for parents. Rather, these grandmas assumed parental duties because of unforeseen, and often tragic, circumstances. A GRG may have legal guardianship or adopt a grandchild and take over all childcare. The grandchild may call this grandma Mommy, a word that makes many grandmas uncomfortable. If so, help the grandchild understand your name is Grandma, not Mommy.

Numbers tell the story of the GRG trend. About 2.5 million grandparents are raising their grandkids each year.[34] Fifty-five percent of the grandmas who are raising their grandkids are under the age of fifty-five. Forty-nine percent of the grandmas raising their grandkids are unemployed. Often, however, other family members are involved. Aunts, uncles, siblings, and older children are also raising youngsters, and many of

---

33 Susan Krauss Whitbourne, "Five Types of Grandparents and How They Shape Your Lives," Psychology Today.
34 Brandon Gaille, "23 Statistics on Grandparents Raising Grandchildren," Brandon Gaille Small Business & Marketing Advice.

these arrangements aren't reported.[35] Statistics on the number of older relatives acting as GRGs are difficult to obtain. This doesn't change the fact that grandmas around the world are raising grandchildren.

Grandparent responsibilities need to be clearly defined, and there are education programs available for them.[36] Both recommendations would benefit GRGs significantly. If you're a GRG, you may get help from Grandparents as Parents,[37] Grandparents Who Care,[38] and the National Center on Grandparents Raising Grandchildren.[39] As mentioned previously, you may also be helped by the Grandparents Raising Grandchildren Worldwide website.[40]

Wise Grandma

The wise grandma is a fount of family wisdom and common sense. Family members and friends come to her for counsel. Helpful as this is, I think the expectations of a wise grandma could become a burden over time. Your grandchild picks up on your wisdom by listening to conversation, observing problem-solving skills, and seeing how you approach life. A wise grandma knows when to kick back and have a good laugh. I think another way to think of a wise grandma is as a sharp grandma.

---

35 Gaille, "23 Statistics on Grandparents Raising Grandchildren," Brandon Gaille Small Business & Marketing Advice.

36 Strom, Robert D., "Building a Theory of Grandparent Development," Arizona State University.

37 http://home1.gte..net/res02two7

38 www.grandparentswhocare.com

39 www.chhs.gsu.edu/nationalcenter

40 www.grandparentsraisinggrandchildrenworldwide.com

Wisdom is often common sense.

Wise grandmas have an abundance of common sense gleaned from years of life experience. Priest and poet John O'Donohue writes about the wisdom of age in his book, *To Bless the Space Between Us*.[41] He describes the times of life when we feel like we're in a strange place, a new and different stage of life. O'Donohue suggests embracing this time. "You look back at the life you have lived up to a few hours before, and it suddenly seems so far away."

Becoming a grandma can make you feel like this. Your past life may seem far away; your new life is uncharted. Yet the wise grandma knows when to keep quiet, when to speak, and when to overlook things. Although wisdom doesn't always translate to power, it can be a powerful tool and used for good. If you're a new grandma, your experience is still valuable. If you're an experienced grandma, you have acquired many skills—skills to share with other members of the Grandma Force. Never underestimate the power of experience because it counts.

Long-Distance Grandma

Whitbourne uses the term "distant grandma" to describe a person who has limited contact with a grandchild.[42] Other resources describe this person as a long-distance grandma, and I prefer this term. Because you live far away, contact with a grandchild may be limited to birthdays and holidays. How can

---

41 O'Donohue, John. *To Bless the Space Between Us: A Book of Blessings.* New York: Doubleday, 2008, p. 49.
42 Susan Krauss Whitbourne, "Five Types of Grandparents and How They Shape Your Lives," Psychology Today.

you close the distance between you and your grandchild? First, you can make technology work for you. Many grandmas are staying in touch with grandchildren via Skype.

While this is an excellent communication tool, you need to learn about Skype and establish some rules for using it. Video chats need to be fun and safe, and if your grandchild has his or her own username, you may want to talk with the child's parents about Internet usage and safety.[43] Chapter 7, "Good Communication, Your Best Tool," focuses on Internet and email safety.

Some grandmas are using video chats to stay in touch with grandchildren as young as sixteen months old. While you may think talking to a child who can barely speak may not be a good use of time, these video chats are a good bonding option for long-distance grandmas. Nina Lewis shares some ideas for video chats with young ones in her article, "Skype With Grandchildren."[44] Her ideas include showing magazine pictures one at a time; saying nursery rhymes; reading nursery rhymes; singing a song; pointing to eyes, ears, nose, etc.; reading picture books; blowing bubbles for a grandchild to watch; and playing games. Keep it short, Lewis advises, and it is good advice.

Long-distance grandmas send written letters to their grandkids. Receiving a letter from grandma is an exciting experience. One letter can become two, then three, and then a pen pal relationship. Journalist Stu Feinstein thinks a written letter is a personal gift for a grandchild and considers letter-writing as a lost art.[45] Feinstein writes from experience because

---

43 Toni Birdsong, "To Skype or Not to Skype: What Parents Need to Know About Video Chat," Securing Tomorrow.
44 Nina Lewis, "Skype with Grandchildren," Grandma Ideas.
45 Stu Feinstein, "Letter Writing is a Lost Art: Grandparents Should Revive It," Grandparents.com.

he sends letters to his nine-year-old grandson. He thinks pen pal letters are an adventure with no boundaries or rules that keep each writer from asking questions.

"We can discuss anything that's meaningful to us," he explains, "and create our own road map and always take the scenic route."

Letter writing has helped his grandson handle fears and share his deepest thoughts. Feinstein says he could write an entire book about what he learned from his grandson. He enclosed one of his favorite books, *Ferdinand the Bull*, with one letter. Writing letters became an extension of the grandfather-grandson relationship. Although a letter can't replace a hug, or kiss, or looking into a grandchild's eyes, Feinstein says it can nurture the spirit. "Each letter is a small treasure to be tucked away, a magical reflection of a moment in time."

Are you a letter-writing grandma? If not, these ideas will get you started. Instead of snail mail, you may choose to keep in touch with your grandchild via email.

1. Share some thoughts about one of your favorite meals. Maybe you had spaghetti for dinner and it reminded you of the time you ate spaghetti with your grandchild. You may still be laughing about the noodle slurping contest you had.

2. Tell about the book you're reading. A teenage grandchild will remember the title, a younger grandchild will remember the topic. You may be reading a book about gardening, bird watching, or collecting toy cars. Tell your grandchild why you like the book.

3. Update your grandchild on what's going on at your place. Maybe you bought a rocking chair or hung a bird feeder

from the tree in the backyard. My granddaughter was pleased when I had two chairs reupholstered in orange fabric because orange is her favorite color.

4. Update your grandchild on what's going on in your town. Maybe there is a new grocery store, movie theater, or park. You could describe the park features, such as a skate boarding track. Envisioning the park gives a visiting grandchild something to look forward to when she or he comes to visit.

5. Write about what you are doing. Dull things like cleaning windows (a heck of a job) and more interesting things like baking chocolate chip cookies, give your grandchild a word snapshot of your life. You could enclose the recipe for chocolate chip cookies with your letter.

6. Talk about holiday preparations. The Banbury Tarts are in the freezer, the packages are wrapped, the cards are addressed. News like this links your child with family. End this letter with, "I can't wait to see you!"

A long-distance grandma has to figure out what type of communication works best for her as she builds a relationship with her grandchild.

Working Grandma

I've been a working grandma for decades. From the moment the twins moved in with us, I continued to write. I had to get up an hour earlier than normal to do this. From five until six, I wrote new copy, and then stopped to fix breakfast for the twins. After they left for school, I resumed writing. We had an in-house network and the printer was in my lower level office. When the twins came to get their print-outs they saw me working at the computer. They saw me working at the computer when they came home from school. They saw me working at the computer after dinner.

Being able to work at home is a blessing, and I'm grateful for it every day. The twins are impressed that I'm still working. My grandson lives in Rochester and is my technical help. My granddaughter lives in St. Paul, manages my website, and takes photos when I need them. All my author head shots were taken by my granddaughter. And my surviving daughter indexed my recent books. The help I receive from family members helps me to keep working.

Getting older doesn't mean your abilities decline. Rather than sitting around, grandmas are making use of their experience, confidence, and productivity. You may keep working to qualify for retirement income, achieve a personal goal, or because you need the money. Rosalind C. Barnett, PhD, and Caryl Rivers discuss working grandparents in a *Psychology Today* website article.[46] Longevity is one reason grandparents are still working. "The startling fact is that the only age group in which labor force participation is growing is workers over 55—in contrast to the steady decline among younger workers," they explain.

Too often, however, a working grandma is a guilty grandma. Keep in mind that your work ethic and diligence can be positive things for a grandchild to see. You look and act like a productive grandma. Children pick up on things, and your grandchild can tell if working makes you happy. I keep writing because it makes me happy.

A working grandma may have a demanding job that requires

---

46 Rosalind C. Barnett and Caryl Rivers, "Why Your Grandmother is Still Working," Psychology Today.

constant vigilance and learning. Continuing education may be required to keep a job. Work hours and continuing education hours may limit the time a working grandma can spend with a grandchild. Talk with parents and see if you can find a regular time, such as every Sunday, to spend with her or him, whether in person or on a video chat. This should make scheduling easier. This plan gives your grandchild—and you—something to anticipate.

The Nanny Granny

The nanny granny is a growing trend, according to author Cynthia Ramnarace.[47] She points out that Michelle Obama's mother was a nanny granny and moved into the White House to help care for the Obama's daughters. You may move in with the family or have your own apartment above the garage. Nanny granny families may sell homes—theirs and the grandmother's—in order to buy a larger one for the family. Parents may put an addition onto the house for Grandma. Construction companies are building "granny units," scaled down outbuildings with kitchen, bathroom, and bedroom.

Nanny granny hours vary from family to family. You may provide help on weekdays, weekends, or all the time. About 6.2 million American grandparents have moved in with their adult children, a throw-back to earlier times. When I was growing up, it was common for a single grandparent (widow or widower) to live with the family. An unmarried aunt would live with the family too. She would help with child care when necessary and contribute to family income. This was the way things were done back then. Contemporary grandmas are embracing the nanny

---

47 Cynthia Ramnarace, "The Nanny Ganny Phenomenon," AARP.

granny role because it helps them know their grandkids. The arrangement is also rewarding. A friend of mine cared for her grandchildren. I met her in a coffee shop, sitting at a table, and bottle-feeding a baby.

"Hi, Jane. I haven't seen you in a while. Are you babysitting today?" I asked.

"No," she answered. "I told my daughter I'd take care of her children until they go to kindergarten."

"That's a long time," I replied.

She nodded her head and smiled. "My daughter and son-in-law need me," she explained, "and I'm glad to help."

As it turned out, my friend cared for four grandchildren. She is one of millions of grandmas who care for grandkids full-time, part-time, or on weekends. Being involved in family life is the new normal for grandmothers, and their tasks include babysitting, daily care, weekend care, driving service, grocery shopping, meal preparation, and respites for parents. Despite good intentions and kind people, being a nanny granny can go awry.

One grandma agreed to be a paid nanny granny and work Monday through Friday. She continued to live at home and drove to the house each day. Her duties included cooking, laundry, cleaning, and chauffeur service. This arrangement worked well until family members started to take Grandma for granted. On a summer day the family went to the beach while Grandma stayed home to make dinner. Family members returned late in the afternoon, walked in the door, and dropped their sandy towels on the floor so Grandma could wash them.

"They treated me like the maid," the grandma later explained. "I was so hurt. That's when I knew I couldn't do this anymore."

Speak up for yourself if you feel like you're being taken for granted. Asking for a family meeting may help to clarify things. Discuss your original arrangement as a nanny granny. How many days do you work? What are your hours? Are you paid or compensated in another way? You may wish to stop being a nanny granny and try something else.

Other Types of Grandmas

The types of grandmas that I've discussed aren't the only ones. When I was surfing the Internet I came across "Different Types of Grandmother," posted on the Gransnet website.[48] The article was adapted from a book called *The Great Granny Guide*. Some types didn't sound good to me, such as the Mad Granny and Granny from Hell. Other types, like the Rock 'n' Roll Granny, Sporty Granny, and Super Granny, made me smile.

While I'm not the Rock 'n' Roll Granny and never will be, I admire this grandma's gumption. She makes no concessions to age, status, or lifestyle, and dresses like a hippy from the past. She may smoke and drink and love junk food. Daughters and daughters-in-law may cringe at this grandma's behavior, according to the article, but forgive her behavior because the grandkids love their grandma. This type of grandma provides endless fun and can be a source of wisdom. Ask this grandma a question and chances are you'll get an honest answer.

The Sporty Granny radiates energy and plays golf, tennis, or other sports. She may come straight from the golf course, tennis court, or swimming pool. Like the fun-seeking grandma, this grandma plans events to involve grandkids in sports and "get them off to a good start." A grandchild may play tennis, take swimming lessons, or try out for the football team or

---

48 "Different Types of Grandmother," Gransnet.

cheerleading squad. While these things can enrich a grandchild's life, sports shouldn't take up too much of a grandchild's time. A grandchild still needs to study and have time for after-school activities.

The Supergran scares me a bit. This type spends countless hours with a grandchild. She devotes tremendous energy and effort to make her grandchild's life better. But as with most things in life, it's the quality of attention, not the quantity, that counts most. I think the Supergran could run the risk of becoming a perfectionist grandma. A Supergran who is a perfectionist can be a daunting combination for the family and your grandchild.

When I was little, there were no grandma types, just grandmas. Often families lived closer together than they do now. Each grandma was a super woman and did what "ordinary" grandmas do. Grandma cooked meals for her family, sewed clothes or knit sweaters for grandkids, babysat when needed, and acted as the family matriarch. It may seem like grandmas were taken for granted back then, but they were not. Grandma was an integral part of the family. Sunday dinner at Grandma and Grandpa's house was a highlight of the week.

Frequent contact with Grandma enabled a grandchild to know their grandma, something that's not always true today.

What type of grandma are you? Some styles may overlap. Before John and I went on a trip, I made all the arrangements and created travel packets for each family member. The packets contained airline tickets, schedules, and event tickets. As the twins went through their packets, my granddaughter said, "I'd like Grandma to arrange all my trips." In this instance, I was the fun-loving grandma and an ordinary grandma. At different times in life, grandma types may overlap naturally.

Be your own grandma—your own unique type.

Whatever it is, whatever job you have, you know time is fleeting. Spend as much time with your grandchild as possible. Sally Wendkos Olds, author and grandmother of five, notes in *Super Granny*, "We know how fast children grow up."[49] The time you spend with each grandchild is a precious interlude, and you want to savor it. Whether you're the nanny granny, working grandma, long-distance grandma, wise grandma, grandma raising grandchildren, or formal grandma, there's only one grandma in the world like you!

---

49 Sally Wendkos Olds. *Super Granny: Great Stuff To Do with Your Grandkids.* New York: Sterling Publishing Co., 2009, p. xiv, xiii.

CHAPTER 5

Part of the Family

Learning to be a Grandma
Family Identity and Values
Their Rules and Yours
Cell Phone Rules
Sharing Chores
Who's in Charge?
Keeper of Stories and History

I have a BS degree in early childhood education, yet there were things I had to learn or review as I raised the twins. You may need to learn new things as well.

Members of the Grandma Force aren't
afraid to keep on learning.

Jasmin Tahmaseb-McConatha, PhD, wrote about her struggle to figure out her role as a grandmother because her responsibilities weren't clear.[50] The grandma role is an evolving one, according to the author, and learning it required a reconstruction of identity. That was okay. Becoming a grandma

---

50 Jasmin Tahmaseb-McConatha, "Learning to be a Grandmother," Psychology Today.

deepened her happiness and made life sweeter. This chapter will help you maneuver the ever-changing role of grandma as it evolves and changes with time.

Learning to be a Grandma

Being a grandma means you have relationships with your grandchildren, and as they grow, your relationship with them changes. The changes can be confusing when they require you to constantly reconstruct a relationship. Reconstruction isn't easy and leads you in surprising—and at times upsetting—directions. You may not be able to convince your grandchild to wear a winter jacket although snow is forecast. Or a grandchild that used to love baking with you as a ten-year-old won't come near the kitchen as a fourteen-year-old. These changes can sidetrack new and experienced grandmas.

As your experience grows, you learn to ignore small changes and stay focused on what's most important. Your grandchild gets used to you, your personality, routine, cooking (or take-out), approach to problem-solving, and how you respond to crisis. Though I had experienced the teenage years with two daughters, I had to re-learn how to be a grandmother to teenagers. This involved learning the latest jargon.

When my grandson asked me if his friend could come over and "hang," I agreed, though I didn't know what "hang" meant. Five minutes later a tall young man walked in the door for dinner. I had prepared dinner for four, not five, and opened some canned soup to accommodate our guest. He hung for dinner. He hung after dinner. He hung all night. He hung for breakfast. He hung for lunch. Teenagers eat more than grandparents and I needed to go to the grocery store.

"How long is he staying?" I whispered to my grandson.

"Don't worry about it, Grandma," he replied.

A few minutes later the young man walked out the door. I hadn't meant to chase him away, and I still feel terrible about it. Since then, I learned that teens who come and stay for a day or several days are often homeless. While this made me feel worse, I had learned something, and now understand the meaning of "hang."

Family Identity and Values

Elisa Medhus, MD, writes about identity in her article, "The Importance of a Strong Family Identity."[51] All family members—parents, children, grandparents, in-laws, and the folks my family jokingly calls the outlaws—help to create family identity. Medhus thinks a strong family identity makes grandchildren more comfortable and acts as a protective shield. Family identity can help a grandchild resist bad influences and peer pressure—or, as Medhus puts it, protect a child from what can be a harsh world.

Medicine is the Hodgson family identity. My father-in-law was a physician and specialized in diseases of the chest. My brother-in-law, a retired physician, specialized in endocrinology. My other brother-in-law earned a PhD in genetics. My husband John, also retired, specialized in aerospace medicine and internal medicine. My niece is a surgeon and head of surgery at a Wisconsin hospital. Much of our dinner table conversation is about past, present, and future medicine. Our grandson is a student at the Mayo Clinic School of Medicine and will be the third physician in our immediate family.

Other factors contribute to family identity. Friends have

---

51 Elise Medhus, "The Importance of Strong Identity," Struggling Teens.

commented on the loving and respectful relationship that John and I share. I didn't know our closeness was that apparent to others. "We love each other, but not like you and John love each other," a friend commented. I was bowled over by her honesty. Our loving relationship was, and continues to be, the foundation of our grandfamily. Other friends have commented on our closeness and, to them, love is part of our family identity.

The twins benefited from our extended family identity of support and love. They remember spending time with extended family members for Thanksgiving dinners, Christmas dinners, overnights, and trips. Most importantly, they remember the support they received from the extended family after their parents died. Family means so much to them and to us. Members of the extended family "have our back," as the saying goes. Maybe that's because family members share the same values.

What are family values? The term refers to how family members live their lives. Values can be formally taught or learned informally.

Amy Guertin, a licensed family counselor, groups family values into six categories: social, political, religious, work, moral, and recreational.[52] She cites examples for each category. Generosity is an example of a social value. Patriotism is an example of a political value. Compassion is an example of a religious value. Respect is an example of a work value. Unstructured play is an example of a recreational value. Guertin admits that compiling a list of family values can be a daunting task, but it's a good idea. She thinks the process should begin with a family meeting. Since this isn't always possible as a grandparent, you may make a list of what you value.

Education is a core value for the Hodgson family, and many

---

52 Amy Guertin, "List of Family Values," Love to Know.

family members have graduate degrees. This value has been transmitted to the next generation. Can you identify a core value for yourself and/or family? Take all the time you need to answer this question. One value may be replaced by another and another as you brainstorm. You may be surprised at the core value you finally choose.

Guertin thinks family values should be in writing. You may handwrite your list or create a computer file. Family values are a work in progress and "may grow and evolve over time, just as your family changes," Guertin says. Talking with other grandmas can give you some insights on family values. You may have more values in common with other grandmas than you first realized.

Raising the twins made me more aware of our family values: always do your best, get an education, keep setting goals, work toward them, always be kind, respect nature, and help others. When I think of family values, I think of a large ship with a sturdy anchor. The anchor is always deployed and helps to keep children from drifting into dangerous waters—skipping school, bullying others, hanging with a rough crowd, trying risky behaviors, experimenting with drugs, and more. Family rules reinforce family values.

Their Rules and Yours

Rules help to enforce a family's values and come from basic needs. Parents have rules for their children, and members of the Grandma Force have rules for their interactions with grandchildren. As you read over the rules mentioned in this section, consider which are applicable to you or if you need to come up with your own rules.

A *Huffington Post* blog post lists rules for grandparents.[53] Rule one is to be aware of what *you* are watching on television while a grandchild is present. This is an excellent rule. A young grandchild doesn't need to see war footage or car crashes. Rule two is to be a good sport and not heckle anyone at a game. Criticizing other players is not acceptable behavior. Rule three is not to treat a grandchild like a show pony. Don't dress them up and take them to see a neighbor to "cheer her up," the blog admonishes. Mandatory car seats are the fourth rule, and I agree with it 100 percent. Rule five opposes the old and dangerous practice of giving teething infants alcohol. Don't try to buy a grandchild's life is rule six; a grandchild doesn't need any more crap from a dollar store. (Amen to that.) Finally, the last rule is to go easy on sweets and stick to your bedtime routine. These rules are logical and easy to follow.

Barbara Graham refers to her rules as laws.[54] Graham lives by seven laws and you may wish to adopt them. I kept Graham's concepts and revised the wording of her statements, which I endorse fully.

1. Every grandma has the right to be silent.

2. Although you think of a grandchild as yours, in truth, she or he isn't really yours.

3. Grandmas need to follow parents' rules.

4. Accept your grandparenting role.

5. Be prepared for old issues to surface when you least expect it.

6. You are entitled to have a life of your own.

---

53 "10 Rules Every Grandparent Should Know," *Huffington Post*.
54 Barbara Graham, "7 Unbreakable Laws of Grandparenting," Considerable.com.

7. Sometimes Grandma needs to alter her expectations.

A grandma herself, Graham believes following these laws helps to keep grandmas out of trouble. Of her baby grand-daughter, she writes, "She was mine, but not mine." Natural as the situation was, the realization shocked Graham, and it took her a while to accept it. Graham's realization may be your realization. As you consider Graham's rules, think about the rules you have for yourself and the revisions those rules may need to undergo to meet new circumstances.

Graham's first unbreakable law is the right to be silent, or as she advises, "seal your lips." Offer your opinion when asked. While this can be hard, in the long run it may be one of the best decisions you ever make. You don't have to comment on everything. Family members and I belong to different political parties, for example, and each one is convinced his or her party is best. When my extended family gets together, I don't say a word about politics. I would rather keep my opinions to myself than spoil a family dinner or holiday.

Parents' rules count.

Even if you don't like them, you need to abide by them, unless you feel a rule is unsafe or harmful. Things change and, since you raised your child or children, new research findings have been discovered, and new products have been manufactured. Your ideas may be outdated—something that is hard to admit. Take car seats, for example, which were not around when I was growing up. Modern seats are built to suit a child's age and weight. Special instructions come with each seat and need to be followed exactly.

It's best to accept your role in the family and not fret about competition. Although you may not see your grandchild as often as the other grandma, enjoy the time you have. After all, you and the other grandma have the same goal: a happy, healthy grandchild. These shared goals create a stronger family.

Prepare for old issues to surface, Graham advises. These issues may include faulty childhood memories, complicated step-families, and blended families. Over the years, incidents can seem more important to family members, and stories can be exaggerated and skewed. Rather than starting an argument, you can go with the flow. Later, when things have calmed down a bit, you might have the chance to clarify things. Clarification is worth the wait.

You don't have to give up everything to be a stellar grandma. Every grandma needs her own life. Be yourself and remember Graham's mantra: *I have my life, they have theirs.* Some aspects of your life need to be private. Time away from your grandchild or grandchildren, an afternoon at the spa, or a weekend trip may energize you for the days ahead.

As you settle into the grandma role and as time passes, you will probably need to revise some expectations. Graham says the good news with altering expectations is that you don't have to be in charge anymore. This can be a relief. Nothing is your fault. I laughed when I read "nothing is your fault" because it puts responsibility on others. Think of yourself as a relief pitcher on the bench, Graham advises, someone who is ready and willing to be called to action.

When it comes to family rules, consistency is important, and all family members need to know the rules.[55] Children fare better when rules are followed by all family members, and family members should be on the same page.

---

55 "Why are Family Rules Important for Toddlers and Preschoolers?" Centers for Disease Control and Prevention.

Talk with your grandchild's parents about family rules. Learn which rules are absolute. Ask about rules that have been altered or eliminated. Which rule is the most important? We posted family rules on the refrigerator. I put both family names at the top of the page to encourage the twins to follow the rules. Helen had taught the twins how to do laundry and, since I needed help with this, the laundry rule is first. The last rule is my favorite.

- Change sheets weekly and wash in warm water.
- Clean out dryer lint trap when you're done.
- Tell us when you're low on clothing, supplies, medications, and money.
- Empty bathroom waste basket when it's full.
- List all appointments/events on master calendar.
- Keep us informed of your plans.
- Call immediately if your plans change.
- Tell us when you're low on snacks.
- Fill the car gas tank when the gauge says ¼ full.
- Let Grandma know a day ahead of time if you're supposed to bring food to an event.
- Let Grandma know several hours ahead of time if a friend is coming to dinner and/or sleepover.
- No phone calls, loud music, or drum music after 9 p.m.
- Always remember that we love you and are proud of you.

You may post family rules on the refrigerator like I did or in another central place. Since grandchildren learn through repetition, it's a good idea to repeat rules every now and then.

The number of rules depends upon your grandchild's ability to understand and if she or he is reading. A young, non-reading grandchild needs a few simple rules, and pictures that illustrate the rules. You may draw pictures or cut and paste pictures from magazines.

Many family rules will be determined by the grandchild's parents, as mentioned. When grandchildren stay with you or visit you, you should enforce the grandchild's parents' rules.

If you feel like those rules are lacking, especially regarding cell phones and household chores, you can introduce additional rules to keep your grandchild safe and healthy. Consider talking about these rules with your grandchild's parents.

Cell Phone Rules

According to an article on the Safe Search Kids website, a whopping 77 percent of teenagers ages twelve to seventeen own a cell phone.[56] Fifty-six percent of tweens, kids who are ages eight to twelve, own a cell phone. A shocking 28 percent of teens admitted to texting inappropriate pictures. Before a grandchild comes to visit, you need to share your cell phone rules.

The Grandma Force can help
enforce cell phone safety.

My daughter (the twins' aunt) bought cell phones for the twins when they were about nine years old. She checked with Helen before she did this. They decided that having cell phones would help keep the twins safe. Helen was a composite engineer

---

56 "Cell Phone Safety Tips," Safe Search Kids.

and worked at a manufacturing plant north of the Twin Cities. Each day, she tumbled out of bed at 4:30 a.m., drove to the Twin Cities, worked eight hours, and drove home again. In an emergency, the twins would be able to use their phones to call their mother or a trusted adult. This proved to be a good decision for their family.

Each family needs to determine its own needs, and a grandma needs to abide by the family's decision. Hopefully each family will also set cell phone rules, but if not, you should encourage grandchildren to follow safe cell phone guidelines when they are with you. These guidelines could include turning the phone off at nine in the evening. Child development experts recommend turning off cell phones one hour before bed. This gives your grandchild a chance to slow down, get ready for bed, and get a better night's sleep.

Insist on no texting while driving. Doing this is worse than driving drunk. Distracted driving is the leading cause of teen crashes in Minnesota. Students in ninth and tenth grades are receiving distracted driver education that includes use of a simulator. The simulation shows students just how impossible it is to drive safely while distracted by a cell phone.

I hope distracted driving education will reduce the number of accidents and deaths. One female student, who lived in a nearby town, was so distracted while texting she crashed into the vehicle in front of her and was decapitated. According to rumor, she only texted a few words, but that's all it takes to have a crash. Now her brave, courageous parents go to high schools and tell the story of their daughter's texting while driving. This story is one all high school students need to hear.

Sharing Chores

Sheila Seifert, director of parenting content for the Focus on the Family website and magazine, discusses appropriate chores in a website article. She lists various age groups and appropriate chores for each group.[57] Kids ages two and three can put laundry in a basket or hamper. Kids ages four and five can match clean socks. Kids ages six and seven can feed a pet. Kids ages eight to eleven can learn to use a washing machine and dryer. Ages twelve and thirteen can change light bulbs. Kids ages fourteen and fifteen can help with yard work. Finally, sixteen to eighteen can help with meal preparation.

Doing household tasks with your grandchild can be a bonding experience. A teenager may unload the dishwasher and you may put the dishes away. If you don't have a dishwasher, you can wash the dishes and your teenage grandchild can dry them. While you're doing these things together, the conversation may be about friends, school work, or next week's plans. You may learn about your grandchild's worries, things like yucky lunches and bullying.

Take advantage of the time you spend doing chores with your grandchild. Chores are a good time to share family history and stories. Although your grandchild may not respond, she or he is listening.

Some kids see a need and respond to it instinctively. You are blessed if your grandchild is one of these kids. I felt blessed when I found my grandson sweeping the garage floor. The city had sanded Rochester's roads all winter, and sand stuck to the car tires. Every time I pulled into the garage, more sand was

---

57 Sheila Seifert, "Age-Appropriate Chores: How to Help Kids Be Responsible," Focus on the Family.

deposited on the garage floor. What a mess! Sweeping the floor had been on my chore list for weeks.

"I didn't know you were doing this," I told my grandson. Thank you."

"I like to help," he replied, and kept on sweeping.

Who's in Charge?

Today, there are different kinds of families—multicultural, step-brothers, step-sisters, families headed by the oldest sibling or an aunt, and grandparents raising grandchildren. This kind of family structure requires adaptation to new people, circumstances, and places. While these adjustments can be challenging, they can also be beneficial—a win-win for everyone. Grandchildren can add fun to the family and generate love that wasn't there before.

But problems can develop, and relationships can become prickly. "Who's in charge" may become a routine question. Generations may squabble. Family members may argue over what television program to watch. Teens may argue about who gets to shower first. Tension can get so bad that you want to cover your eyes and ears and give up. Instead, you can ask for help. Answering the "Who's in charge?" question allows family relationships to go smoothly, and lets you focus on what really matters: staying connected to your grandchild.

Parenting expert Debbie Pincus, MS, discusses family discord in her article, "Grandparents and Parents Disagreeing? 11 Tips for Both of You."[58] In an ideal world, grandparents (and grandmas like you) make life easier for parents. However, unsolicited advice is rarely welcome. Don't let a situation like

58 Debbie Pincus, "Grandparents and Parents Disagreeing? 11 Tips for Both of You," Empowering Parents.

this continue for very long because it will damage the family. Pincus shares her tips for keeping the family functioning well. Her first tip is to assume the best and give parents credit for good intentions. Family disagreements come in all shapes and sizes.

Pincus thinks you should avoid critical statements. Criticism casts a dark, negative pall over everything. Dinner may be ruined. Feelings may be hurt. Family members may leave the room. A shouting match may ensue. Asking how you can be of help is a better approach. Focusing on the positives will do wonders for strengthening family relationships. The solutions that emerge may not be ideal, but you're dealing with family, and family means everything.

Be aware of parental boundaries and when they've been crossed. If you unintentionally crossed a boundary, be respectful and courteous when talking with parents. If a parent feels you've crossed a boundary, listen carefully, speak in a moderate voice, and ask for points to be clarified. Family is family and clarifying the confusion will help you come together.

Don't share information unless you're asked. Be aware of timing, Pincus advises, and don't have disagreements in front of children because arguments put them in the middle. This isn't fair to them. Kids don't want to be in the middle and just want everyone to get along and have fun together.

Be clear about what you will do and won't do. Even if you don't agree with everything the parents are doing, trust your kids to raise their kids. When your grandchild is with you, you are in charge, but still follow the parents' basic rules. Discuss what to do in case of emergency. Enter a list of emergency contacts and phone numbers on your smart phone and/or post a written list on the refrigerator. Also post the name of your grandchild's physician and her or his place of employment.

Keeper of Stories and History

You're a keeper of history as a member of the Grandma Force. This is one of your most important tasks.

Family stories are family history.

Your family's history is also documented with public records, census records, church records, wills, and deeds. Other sources include diaries, journals, photo albums, letters, home movies/videos, business records, and artifacts. To document history, you may want to interview your spouse, significant other, or various relatives. Before you set out, do your preparation work. How does this person fit into the family? What are your memories of this person? Find a quiet place for the interview. As soon as you start recording, state your name, the date, and name of the person you are interviewing. Be yourself and don't try to imitate television hosts.

Refrain from asking *yes* or *no* questions because they can stop conversation. A broad question, such as "You attended Livingston Elementary School. What is your best school memory?" Ask short questions to keep the person interested. Listen attentively and, much as you want to interrupt or make a comment, refrain from doing it. Showing photos may spark responses. Finally, let a family member interview you. Although you may not realize it, you are making history every day.

Although family members are a rich source of history, they may not want to share their memories. John's father refused to let us record his fabulous stories. Pampa was a true raconteur and told one story often. We never tired of hearing it.

Pampa was on a train that was going through Wyoming when a snow storm hit. So much snow fell the train stopped on the tracks. Snow continued to fall and eventually covered the train. Passengers learned that Pampa was a physician and came to him for care. He treated the passengers as best he could without any medical equipment or medications. Everyone on the train was snowed in for days. Fortunately, Pampa had a private compartment with a bed. Word of the snowed in train spread and plows came to the rescue. The plows drove over the roof of the train.

Every time Pampa told this story I could see the stopped train in my mind, picture the dark, snow-covered windows, and almost hear the plows pushing snow off the train car roofs. This story is part of our family history. My husband John followed Pampa's example and refused to let family members record his stories. I hope to change his mind. John has had an exciting life and I want to preserve his story for the next generation.

John made an exception for our church's 130th anniversary. He has been a member of the church longer than anyone else, although he isn't the oldest member. Two members of the congregation visited him and recorded some of his church memories with a smartphone.

John and I were keepers of history when we took our daughters and the twins to the Isle of Man, the original home of the Hodgson family. The twins were eight years old when we went, old enough to read, ask questions, and be observant. I made memory books for the twins and we gave the books to them for Christmas. The twins loved their books and they were stored on a book shelf. When the twins were in their twenties, they came across the books. "I have no memory of the trip," my granddaughter admitted. I am glad I made the memory books because they documented family history.

You may make a memory book about yourself for your grandchild. Use a three-ring binder to hold the pages. Include photos, clippings, and captions. Pages may include the date of your birth, place of birth, baby photos, information about parents, your house or apartment, earliest memories, happiest memories, favorite activities, education, hobbies, favorite activities, schooling, your proudest moment, and favorite foods. Slip each page into a plastic protector. Not crafty? Buy a grandma book and complete it.

As a grandma, you have a role in the family no one else can fill. By communicating with your grandchild's parents, you can better understand that role and smooth family relationships, opening the door for new experiences. Because your grandchildren were safe as they followed family rules, you will remember sharing chores and ancestor stories.

When we were on the Isle of Man with the twins and our daughters, I could hardly believe we were there together. Sometimes I had to pinch myself to believe it was true. I felt blessed to be part of the family, to explore our heritage and values. The next chapter tells you how to build and strengthen the grandma-grandchild relationship. Love really is the tie that binds.

CHAPTER 6

Building a Loving Relationship

Attachment Bonding
Qualities of a Good Grandma
Your Personality
A Loving Relationship
Gifts Greater Than Money
Special Needs Grandchild
Belongingness

You were captivated the second you saw your grandchild. The baby was so tiny and so sweet. Maybe the baby had your eyes. Maybe the baby had the family nose. Maybe the baby snuggled against you, a response that made you feel loved and protective at the same time. Wonderful as these feelings were, building an emotional bond with a grandchild takes time, patience, and persistence. This growing relationship with a grandchild is called *emotional attachment* or *attachment bonding*.

Attachment Bonding

According to The Foundation for Grandparenting, the qualities that influence bonding are readiness (you may have waited years to become a grandma), your persistence, and a positive relationship with your grandchild's parents. This sounds good in theory, but real life may be different. When we became grandparents, John had a new and demanding job and, unfortunately, we only saw the twins every few months or so. The lack of frequent contact with the twins delayed our attachment bonding. I felt bad about this because I knew bonding was beneficial.

Attachment bonding helps those involved to feel comfortable with each other. To develop a strong bond, your grandchild needs to feel emotionally close to you, be in regular contact with you, and think of you as a source of support.[59] Another way to explain this is to imagine a grandchild saying, "I'm upset. I'll talk to Grandma."

After we moved back to Rochester, the twins felt comfortable with us, were in regular contact with us, and felt close to us. This didn't happen overnight; it took several months. We often babysat the twins and tried to make them feel at home. John hung a swing from the back deck and built a see-saw for them. I found age-appropriate toys, games, and videos. I stocked up on art supplies, and kept the cupboard stocked.

The grandma-grandchild bond is beneficial to both of you, but you may wonder how to create this bond and wonder if you have what it takes. According to pediatrician Mary Ann LoFrumento, MD, infants can bond with several people in the family. Bonding can also develop with step-grandchildren and adopted grandchildren. LoFrumento says bonding varies within families. With care, the grandma-grandchild bond lasts for years.

However, bonding doesn't always stay strong and hinges on how involved you are with your grandchild. The success

59 Rita Brhel, "The Vital Importance of the Grandparent-Grandchild Bond," The Attached Family.

of your grandma-grandchild relationship depends, in part, on whether you have the qualities of a good grandma. At this age and stage of life, you have many good qualities. You believe in the power of a grandma and are willing to acquire new skills if necessary. What qualities are the most helpful and important?

Qualities of a Good Grandma

In 2016 the Foundation for Grandparenting, publisher of *Grand* magazine, surveyed families to see whether grandparents were an "indispensable part of their family."[60] Seventy-seven percent of those interviewed thought grandparents were indispensable. The survey cited some of the qualities that help grandparents bond with grandchildren, including "being there," altruism, temperament, vitality, and availability.

Research has shown that being an involved grandparent correlates with the increased emotional security of a grandchild. Altruism—having empathy for others and unselfish devotion—guarantees that family members, and the legacy of grandparents, will continue to the next generation. Your efforts won't be in vain.

Temperament is another quality of a good grandma. I've come across grandmothers who were so nervous they talked constantly, moved constantly, chewed their nails, and never relaxed. I've also come across grandmas who were so comfortable they laughed often, joined in grandchildren's activities, and had a good time. These vital grandmas radiated cheerfulness.

Availability is another quality of a good grandma. Findings show that grandmas who live near their daughters had a clearer

---

60 "Characteristics of Effective Grandparents," *Grand*.

understanding of what the grandmother role entails. This may be due to how often daughter and grandmother saw each other. Then too, it may be a woman-to-woman thing. Good grandmas stay the course, even if they live far away.

Take a moment to think about your availability, temperament, altruism, and "being there." What qualities do you think are important to be a good grandma? You may have all or most of these qualities, and a marvelous personality—the kind of personality that engages a grandchild. The minute your grandchild sees you he or she may smile.

Your Personality

Personality can influence attachment bonding. An outgoing grandma (extrovert) smiles easily, makes others feel at ease, and has a ready sense of humor. If you're an extrovert, you most likely readily show affection for your grandchild, are talkative, and get involved quickly. A contained personality (introvert) is typically more reserved, tends to be solitary, and motivated by ideas. If you're an introvert, you act more reserved, may be less open with your feelings, and less involved. It may take an introvert grandmother longer to bond with her grandchild. Ambiverts have a balance of the two personality types, extrovert and introvert. I'm an ambivert personality and you may be one as well.

These personality differences aren't imaginary and have been confirmed by brain studies.[61] Personality types aren't rigid; they are part of a spectrum. The article, "Introvert vs. Extrovert," contains a diagram of the personality spectrum, and it shows ambivert in the middle.

---

61 "Introvert vs. Extrovert," Diffen.

Are you an ambivert, extrovert, introvert, or another type? You may choose to take the Myers-Briggs Type Indicator (MBTI) test to learn more about your personality.[62]

Introduced in 1942, the test was devised by a mother-daughter team, Katharine Cook Briggs and Isobel Briggs Myers. They based the test on the work of Carl Jung, a Swiss psychiatrist. Jung thought there were four psychological types: 1) extraversion or introversion; 2) sensing or intuition; 3) thinking or feeling; 4) judging or perceiving. The Myers-Briggs test is used to determine personality types in those who are fourteen years old and older.

Only highly trained test givers are allowed give the test, which identifies sixteen personality types. Today, mental health professionals are using the test to assess anxiety disorders and depression. You can find a free version of the test online. I took it and came out as a Protagonist. This confused me because a protagonist is the main character in novels and plays. Did my result mean I always wanted to be the star of the show?

In my early years I was a teacher and taught for a dozen years. Now I'm a writer, a job I've had for thirty-eight years. I have no idea how writing fits into the Protagonist personality type. I do know that learning about my personality type helped me understand how I bonded with my grandchildren.

Although personality and character are related, we need to keep them separate. It's possible to have an outgoing personality and lack the character trait of honesty, for example. Character develops over time as each person puzzles it out for him or herself.[63] Traits like honesty, virtue, and kindness are revealed under certain circumstances and with the passage of

---

62 "Myers-Briggs Type Indicator," Medical Dictionary Online.
63 Alex Lickerman, "Personality vs. Character," Psychology Today.

time. Building a loving relationship with your grandchild can bring out your best traits.

A Loving Relationship

How do you develop a relationship with a grandchild? Susan V. Bosak thinks there are five things you can do to foster a loving relationship.[64] Her simple words require focus, action, and follow-through.

First, *feel it*, or be aware of your feelings toward your grandchild. This requires self-observation, introspection, and honesty. You may also be mindful and try to be aware of each moment of the day.

Think about it comes next. You may think about bonding during the day or even in your sleep. Some of my best ideas come to me when I'm asleep. I am blessed to remember these ideas when I awaken. As part of your thinking, consider activities that foster bonding.

Plan it is the third idea. Plan how you will strengthen the bond with your grandchild. Be prepared to change your plans, however. Thanks to my teaching experience, I usually have a Plan B. This trait has come in handy many times. You may make an alternate plan and, if you do, consider the supplies you need to carry it out.

Make time for it. Note family dinners, play times, babysitting times, and holidays on a master calendar. Some days you may just write "free time." Your calendar may become crowded, and that's an indication of a full life.

Enjoy it is the last idea.

---

64 Susan V. Bosak, *How to Build a Grandma Connection* (Whitchurch, Ontario: The Communication Project, 2000), 29, 68-73.

Enjoy your grandchild every chance you get.

This idea makes me think about the television panel discussion I was on and the mother who said she didn't have time to enjoy her kids when they were little. "I was too busy working," she admitted. While I admired her honesty, her comment made me sad. Avoid this mistake.

Bosak fleshes out these concepts in her book, *How to Build the Grandma Connection*, by providing specific examples of how to build the grandma-grandchild bond. Writing a love letter to your grandchild is one way to forge attachment bonding. Before you start writing, think about your grandma role and what you want to say. You may share a funny story or exciting news that involves your grandchild.

A grandchild may share thoughts with you that she or he wouldn't share with parents, so it's important to be an *active listener*. Active listening requires more energy than halfhearted or passive listening. Be on the alert for unspoken ideas. What is the idea behind the words?[65] Make eye contact, nod your head to show you're listening, and don't interrupt. Not interrupting can be hard, but it's best to hold your comments until the end. Repeat a key point in your mind if you're having trouble following the conversation. At the end of the conversation say something reassuring, such as "Thank you for telling me this" or "Wow! You did well." Listening to your grandchild makes them feel valued.

Knowing when to "dial it back" is another tip. This ability usually comes with age. You know when to have fun with a grandchild and when to be serious. You know when to enforce

---

65 Jeff Haden, "9 Habits of People Who Build Extraordinary Relationships," Inc.

rules and when to relax them. You know when a grandchild is tired or hungry or upset. And you know when you are tired and need to slow down to conserve energy.

Gifts Greater than Money

The bond you've built with your grandchild may be strengthened by giving meaningful gifts. Financial expert Dave Ramsey writes about grandparents' gifts in a blog post, "Spoiling Your Grandchildren Isn't Your Right."[66] According to Ramsey, a grandparent's job is to help grandkids grow into solid adults, not to spoil them. For this to happen, you need to ask parents what they would like you to give the grandkids. This means you give up some control. Some parents don't want their child to have a cell phone, for example. Although you can give your grandchild money for a college fund, Ramsey says the best gift is the gift of time.

You may want to give your grandchild something special, such as a family heirloom or something you value. The trick is to find something your grandchild will appreciate. You may give this gift to your grandchild now or make it part of your will.

Gifts of long-term, personal value include photos, photo albums, yearbooks, wedding books, scrap books, journals, diaries, military memorabilia, and vintage treasures.[67] You may need to copy photos. Caption the photos. If you don't know the people, write "unknown." If you know when the photo was

---

66 Dave Ramsey, "Spoiling Your Grandchildren Isn't Your Right," Dave Ramsey website.
67 Denise May Levenick, "Top 5 Family Heirlooms They Actually Want to Inherit," Family Curator.

taken, add the date. I was particularly interested in the idea of giving journals, diaries, and letters.

These memories bring ancestors to life for your grandchild. Marriage and baptismal certificates, land deeds, and property maps may also be welcome. You could pair your gift with a book on the topic. Surprisingly, vintage sewing machines, fishing tackle, and woodworking tools are sought-after treasures. Match your gift to the receiver. Think about your grandchild's interests, hobbies, and possible career. Enclose a note explaining the item and why you're giving it to your grandchild.

When he was a little guy, we realized our grandson was a tinkerer, in the best sense of the word. He liked to know how things worked and fix things that didn't. In 2013 we moved out of our house into a townhome. The thought of clearing out the house we had lived in for more than twenty years, including the garage and attic above the garage, was so stressful I burst into tears. I couldn't climb the precarious drop-down stairs to the attic, so my grandson climbed up and handed me things. He also carried items down and set them on the floor of the garage.

Before we moved, my husband agreed to give our grandson his tools. It wasn't a gift wrapped in pretty paper and tied with ribbon, yet it was a gift my grandson would use. Heirlooms and treasured items connect your grandchild to family. Psychologists call these items *linking objects*. Is there a linking object you want to pass on to your grandchild? This object can reinforce her or his sense of family. Having a sense of family can help your grandchild survive life's challenges.

Special Needs Grandchild

Attachment bonding with a special needs child requires

adjustments. Learning that a grandchild is a special needs child is difficult news to hear. Your pain is tripled—pain for the parents, pain for your grandchild, and pain for yourself. Although the twins weren't special needs grandchildren, they were grieving for their parents and needed all the support we could provide. Seeing the twins in emotional pain was so painful I wanted to sob.

Examples of special needs are Down syndrome, autism, fetal alcohol syndrome (FAS), attention deficit hyperactivity disorder (ADHD), and learning disabilities. A grandchild may have other disabilities such as hearing loss, vision impairment, or epilepsy. Showing love is even more important if your grandchild has special needs.

Learn all you can about your grandchild's special needs. The health section in the public library may contain helpful books, such as *Understanding Your Special Needs Grandchild* by Clare B. Jones, PhD, *Grandparenting a Child with Special Needs* by Charlotte Thomson, *Autism and the Grandparent Connection* by Jennifer Kumins, and *Help! My Grandchild Has ADHD* by Judy M. Kirzner. Talk to other grandmothers with special needs grandchildren. Find a support group for families of children with special needs.

Figure out what you can do together. Gardening may be one thing a special needs grandchild may be able to do with gentle help from you. Modifications to your home may be necessary, such as a wheelchair ramp and raised gardening space.

As a member of the Grandma Force, you may decide to write your own book about developing a relationship with a special needs grandchild. Information is available from national organizations such as the National Autism Association, National Association for ADHD, National Down Syndrome Society, National Organization on Fetal Alcohol Syndrome,

Children's Diabetes Foundation, Children's Heart Foundation, Epilepsy Foundation, National Association of Epilepsy Centers, and others.

> A special needs grandchild can learn
> from you and you can learn from them.

You may learn to measure progress in moments or inches. You may learn about the healing power of laughter. You may learn about determination and quiet courage. A friend of mine has a mentally challenged granddaughter.

"I take care of her several days a week," my friend explained. "She is so sweet." When she is with her grandchild, my friend looks happy and laughs readily. Her granddaughter smiles in return.

In addition to spending time with your grandchildren, sharing your experience can help others who have loved ones with special needs. You can do this by being open about the difficulties and successes you've experienced with your special needs grandchild, both in person and on social media. If you have a blog or website, you can tell about your experience with your grandchild, with the parents' permission.[68] If you're a techie grandma, you may turn your grandchild's story into a photo book using an online service. Non-techie grandmas may write their grandchild's story and ask the grandchild to illustrate it. There is a hashtag #theytaughtme that you can include if you share your story on social media. Your story can advocate change.

Parents and grandparents need to be strong for special needs children. Your support is a special gift for your grandchild.

---

68 Michelle Manno, "Tell Us Your Story: Blog to Support Special Needs," Tell Us Your Story website.

What your grandchild needs most is love, and you have endless love to share. Show interest in your grandchild's interests and be a friend.

Belongingness

When you consider all the factors, belonging is the basis of any loving relationship. You feel like you belong with a person and they feel like they belong with you. Belonging is more than just bonding. Belonging provides meaning "over and above the value of others or the help they could provide."[69] So belonging is more than bonding and can increase the meaning of life. If you were asked about people or groups that you feel you belong to, what would you say?

Adam Blatner, MD, writes about belongingness in an article with the same title.[70] The feeling of belonging is a basic need, Blatner says, and includes the complex and life-long need for feeling connected. Just as food is for the body, humans need belongingness as food for the soul, he explains. A grandchild who feels belongingness knows you're always there and ready to help. According to Blatner, people who don't feel they belong fill their lives with stuff to make up for a belongingness deficit.

Nothing helps resolve a belongingness deficit like the genuine love of a grandparent for a grandchild. Every moment you spend with a grandchild is a precious gift. Your gift has many parts, keeping stories and history alive, understanding who's in charge, doing chores together, observing rules (including cell phone rules), the family identity and values, and learning to be a grandma. The relationship you create with your grandchild gives life new purpose. In words and deeds, this relationship is

69 "Sense of Belonging Increases Meaningfulness of Life," PsyBlog.
70 Alan Blatner, "Belonging-Ness," Blatner.com.

a tribute to you—a loving, dedicated, and powerful grandma. Effective communication, the focus of the next chapter, makes the grandma-grandchild bond even stronger—so strong it can't be broken.

CHAPTER 7

Communication, Your Best Tool

Body Language Basics
Voice Quality, Pitch, and Tone
Fostering Communication
Updating Communication
Internet Safety
Email from Grandma
Humor as Communication

Like a stringed instrument, communication needs regular tuning. Some grandmas are natural, confident communicators, whereas others are shy and less confident. Good communication is one of the best tools in your toolbelt. You need to know when to be silent and when to speak. You need to know when to be funny and when to be serious. You need to know when to be gentle and when to be strong. But communication skills can falter when you're hurried, stressed, or ill.

This chapter provides a good opportunity to review your communication skills, including body language, tone of voice, and Internet communication. Let's start with some basics of body language.

Body Language Basics

Body language is non-verbal, conscious or unconscious com-munication that includes posture, gestures, movement, and facial expressions. Only 7 percent of communication skills come from words, and 93 percent come from body language. Ninety-three percent is a huge amount! Never underestimate the power of body language.

When I speak to community groups, I scan the audience constantly to check body language. If I have the attention of the audience, I don't change my body language. If I'm losing their attention, I change the pitch or volume of my voice, add another story, and add more gestures. Since the audience sees my gestures in reverse, I gesture left with my right hand, and right with my left hand. Learning to do this took prac-tice.

Body language may be grouped into two main categories, open and closed.[71] People who have open body language tend to be receptive. People with closed body language tend to be resistant. People who have open body language are expressive, interactive, and hands-on. These same people can become argumentative and use excessive gestures to make points. Standing close to someone who is shaking their fist at you is scary. You wonder if fist-shaking will turn to punching.

What kind of body language do you have? Think about when you talk about something you are passionate about. What does your body do? You may be one of those people who talks with your hands (open body language) or you may keep your hands at your side (closed body language). Communication can be difficult when body language is lacking.

---

71 "Body Language—Open and Closed," Tutorials Point.

You may wonder if the other person understood what you said. "Reading" body language is a detailed, complicated process, and you need to be super observant to understand it. One of the best articles I've read about body language is "30 Body Languages and Their Meanings."[72]

Crossing arms is a defensive gesture and may indicate disagreement, the article explains. Biting nails is a sign of insecurity. When a person puts their hand up to their cheek or pulls their ear they are thinking hard. Furrowed brows are a sign of concentration and, during your lifetime, your brows may have furrowed many times. Tapping is an indication of nervousness or impatience. The following story illustrates this point.

One evening John and I went out for dinner. A young man at a nearby table kept shaking his foot. He was eating with another man (whose back was to us), and although the young man looked relaxed, beneath the table, his foot was shaking. As dinner progressed, the man's foot shook faster and faster. The contrast between above the table and below the table body language was startling. Above the table, the man smiled and conversed and continued to eat. Below the table, the man's foot tapped like a piston in an engine. This was an extremely nervous man, and I wondered why he was so upset.

Reading your grandchild's body language is one way to understand the real message behind their words—or their silence. Your grandchild may be a foot tapper. To find out what's bothering her or him, you have two options: direct and subtle. The direct approach means you come right out and say, "Are you worried about something?" You may take a less direct approach by mentioning the surroundings, what's going on, or

72 Angelica, "30 Body Languages and Their Meanings," EnkiVeryWell.

something reassuring. "We have plenty of time to get there." "Yes, I have snacks for your class."

Some negative gestures include placing fingers or hands together, a gesture that's called *steepling*, which indicates a desire for control or authority.[73] Touching one's nose is a sign of disbelief or lying. These are all negative gestures. Rolling the eyes, something your grandchild may have done or still does, can be an indication of frustration, disbelief, or anger. A grandchild may also use this gesture to represent humor.

Be on the lookout for positive gestures—nodding the head in agreement, standing tall with shoulders back, and standing with legs apart.[74] Other open gestures to watch for are open palms (a sign of honesty, sincerity, and openness), and a slightly tilted head (a sign of interest). Many articles about body language are available online and you may wish to read some of them. As management consultant, educator, and author Peter Drucker once said, "The most important thing in communication is hearing what isn't said."[75]

Voice Quality, Pitch, and Tone

Voice is key to effective communication. Your voice is unique and distinguishes you from others. While the sound of your voice is something you're born with, you can control the tone and pitch of your voice.

Tone refers to how you adjust your voice to various situations. My husband speaks Spanish. He taught me a few common phrases to use when we were in Mexico. A vendor approached

73 Angelica, "30 Body Languages and Their Meanings," EnkiVeryWell.
74 Angelica, "30 Body Languages and Their Meanings," EnkiVeryWell.
75 Karen Friedman, *Shut Up and Say Something: Business Communication Strategies to Overcome Challenges and Influence Listeners*, Santa Barbara, CA: Praeger, 2010, 165.

me in the airport, and I bought something from him. The vendor waited impatiently while I rummaged through my purse and looked for my wallet. "Uno momento, por favor," I said. I must have spoken with a forceful tone because the vendor backed up a few steps.

The pitch of your voice can impact communication more than you realize. In many cultures, such as Chinese, pitch changes the definition of words. In all cultures, pitch changes the meaning of words. A high-pitched voice may be interpreted as fear. A loud voice may be interpreted as anger. Some people use their voices improperly. Teenage girls and young women in my area speak in high, child-like voices, which can reduce credibility, and make them seem immature. Just such a woman worked as a check-out person at a local store.

The young woman's voice was so shrill it could have cracked glass. Her voice could be heard throughout the store. People turned and stared whenever she spoke. Every time John and I went to the store, we commented on the woman's piercing voice. I wondered if family members were used to her voice or annoyed by it. Nice as the woman seemed to be, I didn't think I could spend much time with her because of her voice.

From the moment they are born, babies monitor the pitch and tone of the voices they hear. Parents instinctively talk to babies differently than they do to older children or adults. I watched a mother "converse" with her baby in the grocery store. "We're going to buy some soup," she announced in a happy tone and level pitch. The baby didn't understand her mother's words, yet she smiled and cooed in response to her mother's voice. "Oh, there's the bread aisle. We'll get a loaf of bread." The baby smiled and cooed again. The mother continued to chat quietly to her baby as she went from aisle to aisle. This is how babies learn to talk.

Fostering Communication

Communicating with grandchildren of all ages is important to building a bond with them, as discussed in Chapter 6. Grandmas can communicate with babies like the mother in the store talked to her child. A WebMD article, "Baby Talk: Communicating with Your Baby," says it's important to smile at a baby.[76] Smile when the baby babbles to you. Imitate the baby's sounds. This reassures the baby and makes her or him feel like they're talking. According to the article, many adults use a high-pitched voice when they talk with babies. This mimics a female voice, "which babies the world over associate with feeding and comfort."[77]

If you are with your infant grandchild often, talk to her or him throughout the day. Repeat key words, such as "bottle." Around eight to twelve months, a grandchild can say "mamma" and "dada" and may even say "gamma." Holding the baby's hands, gentle hugs, and rubbing your grandchild's back are also forms of communication. Your grandbaby may drift off to sleep while you're doing these things.

Communicating with toddlers and children up to three years old is different than talking to an infant. One suggestion is to help a grandchild develop a "feelings" vocabulary.[78] The word "sad" is used as an example. Youngsters who learn feeling words feel like their feelings are accepted, the article notes. Giving a running narrative of what you are doing also helps a young grandchild develop their language skills. Here are some sample sentences.

"I'm making lunch for you now."

"I'm taking clothes out of the dryer and folding them."

76 "Baby Talk: Communicating with Your Baby," WebMD.
77 "Baby Talk: Communicating with Your Baby," WebMD.
78 "How to Support Your Child's Communication Skills," Zero to Three.

"I'm getting out your special blanket because it's nap time."

"I'm putting your jacket on because it's cold outside."

Language development is a wonderful thing to see. I kept a baby book for our elder daughter, Helen. She began cooing when she was nine weeks old. At ten months, she said "hi" and talked nonsense to herself for a long time in bed. I kept a separate list of the words she learned and the order in which she learned them. Unfortunately, the list disappeared in one of our many moves. You may enjoy keeping a written record of your grandchild's new words.

Preschool and kindergarten grandkids know many words. At this age the number of feeling words has increased. You can help your grandchild learn more feeling words. Writer and editor Lexi Walters Wright shares ingenious ways to foster language development in her article, "10 Ways to Improve Your Grade-Schooler's Communication Skills."[79] One idea is to use conversation starters, such as "What was the funniest thing you saw in school today?"

Reading together is another idea that promotes language development and, more importantly, brings you together physically and emotionally. Take turns reading with your grandchild, Wright advises. Don't worry if your grandchild misses a few words. Wright thinks adults should encourage journaling. "Writing in a diary or journal about day-to-day activities and feelings may help your child [or grandchild] form thoughts to share with others." You can promote journaling by buying a blank journal for your grandchild.

Middle school kids start to think about privacy and may be reluctant to share their thoughts. It's possible to respect your grandchild's desire for privacy and still foster

---

79 Lexi Walters Wright, "10 Ways to Improve Your Grade-Schooler's Communication Skills," Understood.

communication. Wright suggests playing word games (our family loved Scrabble), critiquing movies together, and asking your grandchild's opinion. Continuing to read together is an excellent suggestion. A middle schooler who can read may still enjoy being read to and you could begin with a mystery book.

Communicating with teenagers can be tricky. Researchers say the human mind isn't fully developed until age twenty-five. "Not me" thinking is one of the major flaws of the teenage mind. A teenager may think, *Other teens may run into trouble, but that won't happen to me because I'm smart. I'm the exception.* A partially developed mind isn't going to remember everything you say. While you don't want to act like a preachy grandma, you need to communicate with your grandchild, and keep communicating.

Katie Omohundro, a contributing writer for the *Washington Times Herald*, offers tips for doing this in her article "Five Steps to Better Communication with Your Teen."[80] Her first step is to change your mindset. Be flexible and try to approach the topic from a teen perspective. Think back to when you were a teenager and the feelings you had at that age. Adolescence is a quirky time of life, Omohundro notes, and it's best to let a teenager grow up and start making their own decisions.

Rather than micromanaging, Omohundro recommends coaching. In my experience, a teenager may welcome your coaching or ignore it. Their response to coaching depends on your grandchild's personality, what's going on in the moment, her or his mood, what went on in school, the amount of homework, and other variables.

Being real is another of Omohundro's tips. Let your grand-child know how you feel. Share the vulnerable side of your

---

80 Katie Omohundro, "Five Steps to Better Communication with Your Teen," *Washington Times Herald*.

personality and some of your concerns. Your honesty will make it easier for your grandchild to be vulnerable with you. Avoid "when I was your age" stories because teens are more interested in the present than the past. Chances are your grandchild doesn't care if you walked a mile to school or had a paper route.

Validating a teenage grandchild's feelings is another tip. This doesn't mean you agree with your grandchild all the time. However, it does mean you acknowledge your grandchild's feelings. "Validating feelings allows teens a safe place to open up and allows parents (and grandparents) to meet teens where they are," Omohundro writes.[81] Whether you agree with them or not, every grandchild is entitled to their feelings.

Updating Communication

You may need to update your communication skills as your grandchild grows. This benefits both of you. I updated my skills when the twins were in college. This happened automatically and without much thought. College and university courses had expanded the twins' vocabularies, so I added more words to sentences. Many of my word choices had to do with medicine. For me, learning medical words is ongoing.

Having a large vocabulary has many benefits.[82] One benefit is a faster processing speed for the mind. Expressing ideas is easier when you have a large vocabulary. Expanded abstract thinking is another benefit of vocabulary. Words shape thoughts and knowing more words helps you express them. Although

81 Katie Omohundro, "Five Steps to Better Communication with Your Teen," *Washington Times Herald*.
82 "Why a Substantial Vocabulary Is Important," Gray Matter.

we often view thoughts as shaping words,

words shape thoughts.

You can help your grandchild learn new words by adding them into conversation, keeping a list of new words, and choosing a word of the day. You and your grandchild may wish to keep lists of your favorite words.

Success at work is another benefit of an expanding vocabulary. This benefit also applies to school children. Having a large vocabulary can help your grandchild be successful in school. If your teenage grandchild applies for a job, their vocabulary can influence whether she or he is hired. A large vocabulary is the best predictor for career success, the article explains, so encourage your grandchild to learn new words, and keep learning them. Learning new words is helpful only if the words are used.

The twins are in their mid-twenties now. They changed their communication to match mine. My grandson discusses detailed medical issues and uses medical terms that I haven't heard before. My granddaughter talks about what works and what doesn't in marketing. When I asked her how often I should post articles on my blog, she said quality counted more than quantity. We often discuss art, a topic that fascinates both of us. Conversations with adult grandchildren should be enjoyable and respectful.

Internet Safety

The Internet has become a giant vehicle of communication, and it's important to understand the pros and cons of using it. The pros include the ease of communicating over long distances, keeping in touch with many loved ones via social media, and having thousands of years of knowledge at our fingertips. The cons include cyberbullying, viruses, and inappropriate content that is easy to access.

Today, many grandchildren are staying in touch with Facebook, Twitter, and other social websites. As a member of the Grandma Force, you need to protect your grandchild from cyberbullying. The Children's Online Privacy and Protection Act (COPPA) was written to help children who are younger than thirteen when they're online. Websites are required by law to explain their privacy policies. The law requires websites to get parental consent before collecting or using a child's personal information.[83]

You may adopt the parents' Internet guidelines as your guidelines. These guidelines could involve not allowing Internet access at certain hours or limiting the number of hours a child can be online. While many Internet and computer usage rules depend on family circumstances, in my opinion, three rules are absolutes and non-negotiable.

Absolute rule one: Never let a grandchild post a photo of themselves or request a photo from someone else. This rule applies to baby photos and group photos. Too many stories have surfaced lately about pedophiles. You don't want to attract these people to your computer or grandchild. The person who sends or requests a photo may use a fake personal photo to conceal their identity. Tell this to your grandchild several times. Make your grandchild believe it.

Absolute rule two: Never share personal information. A grandchild shouldn't share their birth date, gender, address, home phone number, cell number, school name, or school

---

83 Ben-Joseph, Elana Pearl, "Internet Safety," KidsHealth.

location. A teenage grandchild shouldn't share information about their new summer job, where they work, or his or her work hours or salary. Talk with your grandchild and stress the importance of this rule.

Absolute rule three: Never agree to meet someone they met on online and don't know. If your grandchild is invited to meet someone, tell the parents. Write down the date, time, website, and whether the request was a video or email. Trust your judgment and alert the police if you think it's necessary. Find out if any of your grandchild's friends received similar invitations.

If a grandchild spends time with you, you should be informed of any scary or threatening emails she or he receives. Has this person previously contacted your grandchild? Print out these emails for evidence. These tips are harder to execute as your grandchild gets older. Teenagers want some privacy and that's understandable. Still, adults need to know about the sites and apps teens are using. Grandkids should never share their passwords with anyone—not with a boyfriend, not with a girlfriend, not with a best friend.

Set your computer in a central place. Don't put your computer in a bedroom or room that can be locked. My computer desk is in a wide hallway visible from the front door, living room, bedroom, and bathroom. Family members walk by the computer constantly. Talk to your grandchild about online safety and how to stay safe. Remind your grandchild that people who are online may pretend to be someone else and share false information.

We can help to protect grandchildren
from online predators.

Internet safety doesn't only apply to grandchildren. You need to be careful, too. Jerri Collins writes about protection in a website article, "How Do I Avoid Dangerous Websites?"[84] Grandmas new to the Internet and experienced users should heed his advice. As a general computer safety precaution, make sure your computer has some sort of protection against viruses and malware that often infect a computer if you accidentally go to a dangerous site. Your computer should have built-in protection, and you can consider subscribing to a protection service. Google offers something called "safe search filtering" that you can turn on or off on its Advanced Search page. This feature works for images and videos. Collins says if a user knows how to turn off search engine filters, she or he can bypass them.

Never guess a website address. I've done this and won't do it anymore after reading this article. Guessing gets people into trouble. Many websites have similar addresses. A simple typo can result in visiting the wrong site. One of my family members was trying to find information about the US government. He didn't have a website address, so he guessed at it and wound up on a porn website. Instead of guessing, you can try some search words and see if a website address appears on the screen.

Never click on websites that seem questionable is Collins' next tip. If something doesn't seem right and you are starting to feel suspicious, heed your instincts and find another website. This is the best way to avoid trouble. "Even the safest, most well-intentioned searches can end up in places that searchers didn't mean to go," Collins explains.[85] Don't let this happen to your grandchild or you.

Knowing how to evaluate a website is a handy skill to have and developing it takes practice. You need to be constantly alert.

---

84 Jerri Collins, "How Do I Avoid Dangerous Websites?" LifeWire.
85 Collins, "How Do I Avoid Dangerous Websites?" LifeWire.

As soon as I log into a website, I identify its purpose. I scroll down and check the authors' credentials. Are these authors reliable? I read sample articles to determine if the website is biased. Finally, I check the domain. There are four domain categories: government (.gov), education (.edu), organization (.org), and commercial (.com).

Email from Grandma

Grandkids stay in touch with email. No doubt about it, email is easy and quick. Just like writing a letter to your grandchild, writing them an email has basic etiquette and "Fundamental Email Etiquette: 26 Easy Roles to Follow" by Heinz Tschabitscher spells it out.[86] You can decide which tips will improve your email communication, both with your grandchild and others.

The first piece of etiquette, proofreading emails, is obvious. I've found typos in my emails more times than I want to admit. It's also a good idea to let an email "rest" before sending it. Be aware if you are hitting *reply* or *reply all*. Is your response meant just for the sender of the email, or for everyone the sender sent the original email to? Keep emails short. A short email is more apt to be read. Chances are your grandchild doesn't want to read pages of copy.

Write clear subject lines and format your email properly. To avoid confusion, limit the subject to one topic. Acronyms should be spelled out unless you know the recipient will understand them. Remember, using all capital letters is interpreted as shouting by the person who receives your email.

Call me a suspicious person, but I don't participate in any email surveys or chain letters and think they are a waste of

86 Heinz Tschabitscher, "Fundamental Email Etiquette: 26 Easy Rules to Follow," LifeWire.

time and an invitation to trouble. An Internet scammer may have written the email. The article advises email users to get antivirus software.

Reduce a photo if it's too large to send. This catches me unaware all the time. Let your grandchild know if a photo is on the way. If you have a large batch of photos to send, divide the batch into several emails, and send a few photos at a time. Be sure to include happy and humorous photos if you have them.

Email, like the Internet, is a modern convenience that has made communication easy and instantaneous. As long as you take the necessary precautions, it can be a great communication tool with your grandchild, especially if you are a long-distance grandma.

Humor as Communication

Grandkids respond to humor more than lectures that drone on and on. Adding humor can change an entire conversation.

Humor helps to get your message across.

Speech expert JoJo Tabares cites the pluses of humor in her article, "Humor: A Powerful Communication Tool?" [87] Although the title ends with a question mark, the article praises humor in paragraph after paragraph. "Carefully diagnosed as fun, humor can smuggle new ideas into people's hearts," Tabares writes. There are many advantages to using humor. It brightens the day, and people remember it and re-tell the jokes and stories they hear.

Humor lets you approach threatening topics in a non-

---

87 Jojo Tabares, "Humor: A Powerful Communication Tool?" Creation.

threatening way, according to Tabares, and is a language all cultures understand. Communication improves once a person's defenses have been lowered. Tabares describes humor as a model of efficiency, and I agree with her words. Humor delivers a message in seconds. One funny line can keep a grandchild laughing long after the first laugh.

Using humor in snail mail and email makes your messages appealing. You may share a joke and your grandchild may share a joke. Sharing jokes may become a regular thing. This back-and-forth communication can turn into the Joke of the Week.

Grandmas can use humor to soften harsh messages. As George Bernard Shaw once said, "If you're going to tell people the truth, you'd better make them laugh." Give a cheer for humor and use it often. The laughter you share with your grandchild will be remembered.

Now you know the elements of good communication: humor, online smarts, how to foster communication, a pleasant voice, tone, and pitch, and body language basics. These elements help you successfully "send" messages to your grandchild. When all else fails, try charades. John and I ate dinner at a restaurant in Manheim, Germany. I wanted fish and, since I didn't know German, imitated a fish. The waiter grinned at my opening and closing fish mouth, and flapping arm fins (hands tucked under my arm pits and moving elbows). He got the message and ordered a fabulous fish dinner for me. Good communication will leave you and your grandchild smiling!

CHAPTER 8

At-Home Activities for Grandkids

Reading Aloud, Your First Choice
Successful Sleepovers
Cooking Together
Grandchild's Interests
Art as Personal Expression
Cursive Writing Practice

A grandchild can grow so quickly it can be hard to keep up. One day your grandchild is looking at board books, the next day, or so it seems, she or he is reading novels. You wonder where the time went. How did your grandchild grow so quickly? Your grandchild's developmental changes may lead to questions. You may wonder if your grandchild's development is lagging, on target, or ahead. To answer questions about your grandchild's physical and mental development, check out a book from the library or buy a book.

When you've determined the developmental level of your grandchild, you can create activities that suit her or his level. This chapter offers at-home activities to do with your grandchild. The activities keep your grandchild involved and foster bonding. You can also do most of these activities if you use a cane or are in a wheelchair.

Reading Aloud, Your First Choice

Reading aloud to your grandchild gives you one-on-one time with her or him and, depending on age, a chance to snuggle. According to the American Academy of Pediatrics (AAP), reading to your grandchild is the best way to foster mental development.[88] Working in partnership with the Clinton Global Initiative, the AAP developed "Too Small to Fail" kits to foster early language development. Visit www.toosmall.org for more information about the program and kits.

John and I showed board books to our daughters early in their development. As our daughters grew, the board books were replaced with story books. Our daughters loved *Pat the Bunny* by Dorothy Kundhart. Their favorite page was "Feel daddy's scratchy face," the one with sandpaper on it. Every time John read this page, our daughters reached up and felt the whiskers on his cheek. This book changed our younger daughter's life.

Amy knew the story by heart. As John was reading the book to her one evening, she looked up and announced, "I think I can read." And she could. Countless readings of *Pat the Bunny* helped Amy understand the sounds of letters and how these sounds formed words. She was pleased with herself, and John was thrilled about Amy cracking the reading code. When she started at her new school, Amy wouldn't need to learn phonics because she already knew them.

I took courses on how to teach reading. Although I knew Amy taught herself to read, I didn't follow up on this because we were about to move. I didn't know which reading program her new school used and didn't want to interfere. One thing was

88 Shannon Maughan, "American Academy of Pediatrics Backs Reading Aloud from Infancy," *Publishers Weekly*.

sure: Amy didn't need competing programs. She remembers coming home from school and me asking, "What did you do in school today?"

"I learned to read," she declared.

Of course, Amy didn't learn to read in one day. She learned to read by John and I reading to her to since infancy and constant exposure to books. We all treasured books and our home was filled with them. I bought books for the girls, many of them so beautiful we wanted to keep them forever. Today, Amy loves books and treasures them as much as I do.

Reading aloud is part of a grandmother's job.

You have two goals. One is to help your grandchild become a super reader. The other is to develop your grandchild's love of books. Make story time with your grandchild special by following the tips in "Benefits of Reading to Your Child," posted on the Raise Smart Kid website.[89] I kept the initial ideas and revised the wording.

Find ways to involve your grandchild in reading. Ask her or him to point to colors, or certain animals, or if your grandchild is older, read part of the story. You could take turns reading alternate pages.

Read to your grandchild at the same time of day. In other words, create your own story hour. If you don't see your grandchild often, assure her or him that you will have story hour the next time she or he comes to visit. You could also read to a grandchild on Skype.

Expose your grandchild to a variety of books. This is possible with children of all ages. One time you may read a story about

---

89 "Benefits of Reading to Your Child," Raise Smart Kid.

planes. Another time you may read books about children in other countries. A toddler will enjoy looking at pictures that illustrate the alphabet, pictures of farm animals, and pictures of babies. I've always been intrigued at how much babies like to look at pictures of other babies. Go online to find which books are recommended for which age groups. The children's librarian at the public library can also recommend titles to you. Try to read some of the classics to your grandchild.

Books for children fall into major categories: board books for babies, picture books, picture story books, and traditional books. The latter category has many sub-categories: folk tales, fairy tales, fables, legends, history, fantasy, realistic fiction, nonfiction, biography, poetry, and drama.[90] Picture books don't need to tell stories.

Our daughters loved Richard Scarry's books and we loved them too. John and I read *Cars and Trucks and Things That Go* more times than we could count. Scarry's illustrations were extremely detailed. We all searched for hidden images in the drawings—a bug, worm, or animal with a comical expression. Looking for these things kept us turning the pages backward and forward. This talented illustrator created two hundred books in his lifetime and they are still in print today.

Picture story books have a plot and illustrations. I used to collect picture story books but had to get rid of them before we moved into our wheelchair-friendly townhome. Although I donated the books to the Friends of the Rochester Public Library, giving away the books was painful. My feelings are still painful because I gave away part of myself.

Picture story books are entertaining and teach children new concepts. Shannan Younger details the benefits of reading to

---

90 "Children's Genres," Breitlinks.

children in her article, "7 Reasons Why Reading Aloud to Older Kids is Still Very Important."[91] The first reason may surprise you. A child's brain responds more to words read aloud than words read silently.

Reading aloud to a grandchild helps to boost vocabulary. Reading books above your grandchild's reading level can increase vocabulary. Plus, reading is fun. As Younger points out, you will snuggle less as a child grows, but you can still feel close, and this is a "wonderful side benefit for both parties." Take advantage of story hours in your community. The Barnes & Noble store in Rochester, Minnesota, has story hours for children. The Rochester Public Library has bedtime story hours for young children and they come in their jammies. Many communities have similar programs and you can learn about them on the Internet.

When you go on a trip with a grandchild, bring a book or reading device along. The good thing about a reading device is that your grandchild can order a book from almost anywhere. If you're in a remote place, you may have to shift your location to pick up the signal and download a book. Make books part of your grandchild's life. "Surround your kid with books," the article advises. You may enroll your grandchild in a book club. Give the gift of books on birthdays and holidays.

Successful Sleepovers

Having a sleepover is another at-home activity with your grandchild. Your willingness to host a sleepover can foster bonding with your grandchild. Successful sleepovers depend

---

91 Shannon Younger, "7 Reasons Why Reading Aloud to Older Kids is Still Very Important," Chicago Now.

on planning. Ask your grandchild for input and follow as many of their suggestions as you can.

Lisa Murphy offers idea in her article, "10 Tips for Hosting a Successful Sleepover."[92] She tells grandparents not to host a sleepover until your grandchild is ready for it. If your grandchild isn't ready, plan half a sleepover—wearing pajamas until their parents pick them up before bedtime.

It's wise to limit the number of kids who come for the sleepover. Set specific drop-off and pick-up times. Include a food activity, such as decorating cupcakes or make-your-own ice cream sundaes. Stock up on games and healthy snacks. If you're having a sleepover for teens, be sure to make plenty of food.

Helen had a sleepover for neighborhood friends and I served tacos. I cooked three pounds of hamburger, added seasonings, and put the taco meat in a slow cooker to keep it warm. I set the toppings—lettuce, tomatoes, shredded cheese, sour cream, taco sauce—next to the meat. To my shock, the slow cooker was empty in fifteen minutes. "The meat is gone," Helen announced, "and the girls want more tacos." Fortunately, I had extra hamburger in the freezer. I defrosted the hamburger in the microwave and made another batch of taco filling.

Although kids will want to be alone, stay close by in case something goes wrong. Keep extra tooth brushes, toothpaste, and pillows on hand. Prepare yourself for a short night's sleep because that's what you will get. Your grandkids will be grateful for your planning and love—and extra taco meat—though they may not recognize your efforts until they are older.

---

92 Lisa Murphy, "10 Tips for Hosting a Successful Sleepover," Today's Parent.

Cooking Together

Cooking is a wonderful activity to share with your grandchild. Many memories of Grandma are connected to food.[93] There are lifelong benefits to cooking with grandchildren because cooking involves math, measuring, chemistry, techniques, eye-hand coordination, choosing the right pan, and baking times. Your grandchild also learns about kitchen safety.

Every recipe you make isn't going to be worthy of a five-star rating. For every recipe that you make that is unbelievably yummy, there will likely be one that tastes like sand. Be careful about downloading recipes from the Internet. I've found errors in recipes and think many aren't tested before they are posted. You wind up being the test.

"Why Cooking with Your Grandkids Matters," by Joanna Pruess, says cooking with a grandchild helps her or him learn that food comes from farms.[94] What an important lesson! Since Minnesota is a farming state, the twins understood this concept. There are many farms on the outskirts of Rochester and on the way to the Twin Cities. Grandkids who live in inner cities may be less aware of the origins of food. Pruess thinks too many kids grab food on the fly and think it comes from a fast-food counter. "Making 'real' food can be a small antidote to our national fast-food mania," she writes.

I remember shelling peas in the back yard with my mother. This taught me that peas come from pods. I also remember "Frenching" green beans, cutting them into thin strips with a special tool. New tools have been invented since then, but I prefer to use the type my mother used. I bought it years ago

93 Susan V. Bosak, *How to Build the Grandma Connection* (Whitechurch, Ontario: The Communcation Project, 2000), 70.
94 Joanna Pruess, "Why Cooking with Grandkids Matters," Next Avenue.

and it still works. My mother had a large mint patch in the garden and I learned that mint can add flavor to many foods. She would ask me to go outside and snip mint from the patch, which seemed to have spread every time I saw it.

Pruess considers the kitchen a place of creativity. I'm reluctant to admit this, but I rarely make a recipe as written. Baked goods are the exception because baking is chemistry. I may eliminate an ingredient, such as fennel, which I can't stand, or add an ingredient or two. The twins watched me do this. Cooking encourages originality and personal style, according to Pruess, and over time, this builds trust between grandma and grandchild.

While you're cooking together your grandchild may share information, even secrets, with you. Your grandchild may begin to rely on your expertise in the kitchen. Before my grandson moved into his college apartment, I compiled a list of essential kitchen items for him. Years later I was surprised to learn he saved the list and used it to stock his apartment after graduation.

What should you make together? While cookies may be the first thought that comes to mind, consider pretzels.[95] Slicing fruits and vegetables (depending on your grandchild's age) and helping to make an entire meal are other ideas for what to prepare.

My grandson loved my lemon chicken and watched me make it several times. He asked if he could help and I said, "Sure." He pounded chicken into thin pieces, dipped it in beaten egg, then dipped it in Italian bread crumbs, and carefully slid the pieces onto the cast iron skillet. Later he asked me for the recipe and I told him there wasn't one. Making lemon chicken is more a process than a recipe, and now he knows the process. You may

95 Susan V. Bosak, *How to Build the Grandma Connection* (Whitechurch, Ontario: The Communcation Project, 2000), 70.

share recipes with your grandchild. This is fun if you're a long-distance grandma.

Eating together as a family is one of the best gifts you can give a grandchild—a time to gather together, savor good food, and share stories.

Many cookbooks for children have been published. Although a book may be attractive, check to see if it is really a cookbook. Putting celery arms and carrot legs on a skinny sandwich isn't cooking, it's assemblage. Share the basics if you're going to cook with your grandchild: measuring, safe cutting, pan sizes, temperature, etc. I made cookbooks for my grandkids when they were in college. I typed their favorite recipes, inserted them in page protectors, put the recipes in a three-ring binder, and slid a cover page into the front pocket. The name of my cookbook was *Grandma's Kitchen: Tasty Recipes for Busy Grandkids.*

Grandchild's Interests

Try to support your grandchild's interests. Your grandchild will appreciate your interest and, as time passes, will be grateful for your support. You may need to become Grandma the Detective to spot these interests. Figure out what kind of books your grandchild likes best. Listen for conversational clues. Your grandchild may talk about trucks, point to trucks, and play with trucks more than other toys. An older grandchild may ask to see an adventure movie or attend a ball game. These are obvious clues. Others may be less obvious.

My grandson had his late father's guitar. Years ago, his father found the guitar in a pawn shop and bought it. The Gibson guitar had good tone. John and I could hear our grandson strumming the guitar in his bedroom and trying different chords. We decided to give him guitar lessons for Christmas. I took the guitar to a music shop, and the owner's eyes brightened when he saw it. "I know this model," he said and strummed a few cords. "It's a classic and quite valuable." I asked the co-owner if the non-electric guitar would work for lessons and his answer was yes.

We gave our grandson a beginning guitar music book for Christmas and a note that said he was entitled to beginner's lessons. The first two lessons went well; the third lesson, not so well. I think the instructor was using pot or was very ill because he couldn't keep his eyes open, had difficulty making sentences, and couldn't follow our conversation. Every time we saw him, he acted this way. My grandson lost interest in guitar lessons, and we lost interest in paying for them. Still, our grandson had a chance to use his father's guitar, an object that linked him with his deceased father.

Robert Myers, PhD, assistant clinical professor of psychiatry and human behavior at the University of California, writes about children's talents in his article "4 Ways to Spot and Nurture Talent in Your Child."[96] His tips may be applied to grandchildren. The first tip is to be on the look-out for talent. When you discover your grandchild has talent, nurture it as best you can. Background enrichment, taking every opportunity to broaden and enrich your grandchild's understanding, is important.

One way to discover your grandchild's talent or talents is to expose them to different kinds of activities. The Rochester Symphony and Chorale hosts an annual introduction to musical instruments called "Honk, Squeak, Scratch, and Boom." The event is for fourth, fifth, and sixth grade students who have

96 Robert Myers, "4 Ways to Spot and Nurture Talent in Your Child," Child Development Institute.

expressed an interest in music. They get a chance to try various instruments, and this helps them decide which instrument they would like to learn. Look in the local newspaper or online to see if your community has similar events that would interest your grandchild.

Myers thinks talent is worth pursuing only if a child can enjoy it. He goes on to say that being a champion chess player wouldn't enrich a child's life if she or he found competitions unbearably dull. After you've put emotional and financial effort into supporting a grandchild's interests, their interests may change. That's life. That's a grandma's life. Whether or not your grandchild becomes a concert or amateur pianist doesn't change the love you feel for your grandchild.

Art as Personal Expression

Art is a wonderful, far-ranging activity to do with a grandchild. One advantage to art is that it's adaptable. If you have a chronic illness, or caught a cold, you can still provide materials for your grandchild. Designate a drawer as your grandchild's art drawer and stock it with water color markers, crayons, rubber stamps, plain paper, colored paper, glue sticks, Elmer's glue, (which is milk-based), age-appropriate scissor, collage materials (stickers, bits of fabric, lace, ribbon, yarn, etc.), and box of water colors.

Store art materials in a plastic basket if you don't have an empty drawer. I'm not a fan of coloring books or asking kids to color within lines. This isn't self-expression. Drawing on blank paper is self-expression.

> Artwork reveals your grandchild's
> personality and thoughts.

Old-fashioned as they may seem, crayons are still a wonderful medium for grandkids. A nursery school age grandchild or kindergarten age grandchild will enjoy making crayon cookies. You can make them together. Heat the oven to 200 degrees. Peel the paper off stubby crayons and break them into small pieces. Drop the pieces into a foil muffin pan or regular pan lined with paper liners. You need about an inch of broken crayons in each cup. Put the pan in the oven.

When the crayons have melted and merged, remove the pan and cool on metal rack. Remove the paper liners from the crayon cookies and store in a plastic container until a child wants to color with one. Crayon cookies are a fun way to recycle old crayons.

One of my nursery school students loved to paint at the easel. He always painted the same thing, straight lines of various colors that went across the paper or turned a corner. There were no curved lines in his paintings. Instead of asking "What is it?" (which can hurt a child's feelings because the child knows what it is and assumes you do too), I began with, "I love the colors you chose. Can you tell me about your painting?"

Steven didn't answer. He was deep in thought and had work to do. On the last day of nursery school, Steven painted a large square in the middle of the paper.

"Tell me about this shape," I said gently.

Steven grinned. "It's the sink," he announced.

I finally understood. He had painted pipes all year and now had connected them to the sink! I was speechless. Ever since then, I've wondered about what happened to Steven. Did he become a plumber, an engineer, or an abstract artist like Piet Mondrian? Maybe he became a physician like his father.

The nursery school I worked at respected children's artwork so much that teachers never folded paintings. Each painting was carefully rolled and taped closed with masking tape. Many parents framed their children's art work. Framing and displaying your grandchild's artwork shows you value it. You can find inexpensive frames at garage sales for a few dollars. Craft stores have sales on frames. (You may need a coupon.)

I saved samples of the twins' artwork for several years and made memory books for Helen's birthday. Each twin had their own book. My granddaughter's book begins with a red crayon scribble drawing and the scribbles bounce wildly over the paper. Several pages later, there is a circular orange drawing with two blogs of color at the top. The caption reads, "It's a face." Other drawings in the book include "Smiley sun and man," a sun shining over a flower, and a drawing of an apartment house with two tall towers, and ladders instead of stairs. One of the most amazing drawings is a line drawing for the deaf hand sign that means "I love you."

You may compile a similar memory book of artwork. A three-ring binder works as well as a scrapbook and, when filled with your grandchild's artwork, can be displayed on a coffee table.[97] Don't fold a large drawing because it destroys the picture, and your grandchild knows this. Instead, display artwork on the refrigerator.

Drawings can be laminated and used as placemats.[98] You may photograph artwork with a digital camera and display pictures in an electronic frame. Designate a small wall or the back of a cupboard as your grandchild's display area. Hiding artwork for your grandchild to find is another idea, such as putting a small drawing under a pillow. Your grandchild's artwork can also become a T-shirt or coffee mug decoration.

97 Felicia Bollet, "9 Crafty Ways to Display Grandkids' Art," Grandparents. com.
98 Bollet, "9 Crafty Ways to Display Grandkids' Art," Grandparents.com.

Art projects scare some grandmothers. "I can't draw a straight line," one complained. Don't worry! There are many ways to appreciate art, and many types of art to appreciate. Drive past historic buildings in your town and talk about why you like them. Watch a new building go up and talk about the progress. Look at outdoor sculpture or a sculpture garden.

Cindy Ingram manages the website The Art Curator for Kids of All Ages, which has a resource library, workshops, podcasts, and blog. Ingram's mission is to take art out of the dark, eliminate sleepy classrooms and replace it with "meaningful, rigorous, and fun art learning." You can subscribe to her free newsletter and download a finish-the-picture art game for your grandchild. Each game page has part of a famous painting on it and your grandchild finishes the painting with the medium of his or her choice. Adults would enjoy this game. In addition to free art projects, Ingram has a membership program devoted to teaching art history and appreciation.

A preschool or kindergarten child will enjoy these picture books about art.

- *Harold and the Purple Crayon* by Crockett Johnson
- *The Line* by Paula Bossio
- *Henri's Scissors* by Jeanette Winter
- *Swatch: The Girl Who Loved Color* by Julia Denos
- *Little Blue and Little Yellow* by Leo Lionni
- *The Day the Crayons Quit* by Drew Daywait
- *The Dot* by Peter H. Reynolds.

A teenage grandchild will enjoy novels about art. I just finished *The Art Forger* by B. A. Shapiro and was enthralled by it. Your grandchild may also enjoy *Artist to Artist: 23 Major Illustrators Talk to Children About Their Art* by Eric Carle. Benefits from book sales go to The Eric Carle Museum of Picture Book Art. This is one of those books that's appropriate for children and adults, and I bought it for my artistic daughter. Each illustrator has a page that folds out. There's even a pop-up illustration.

Be smart about art. To protect their clothes, a preschool or kindergarten grandchild should wear an apron, plastic smock, or men's shirt with rolled up sleeves. Lay newspaper, an old sheet, or cheap plastic tablecloth under your grandchild's work space. A grandchild shouldn't use Sharpie markers in a closed space because they contain a dangerous inhalant. I had my nursery school students draw with Sharpies, but we did it in the spring when we could open the classroom windows and get cross ventilation. The kids only used the markers for a few minutes and switched to water colors.

Art projects give your child a chance to express herself or himself and give you opportunities to spend with your grandchild. This quiet time, as opposed to a crowded playground or blaring television program, is an ideal time to bond with a grandchild.

Cursive Writing Practice

Practicing cursive writing is another at-home activity to do with your grandchild. I was taught the Palmer Method of cursive handwriting and, in my mind, still see the green alphabet posters on the classroom walls. To me, the posters looked like a marching alphabet army, and I stared at them for hours. Maybe I stared too much. The way I write the letter *r* goes back to that poster, and I can see the strokes in my mind. Some people can't read cursive, a fact I discovered accidentally. A friend asked me to jot down an address. I complied and handed the paper to her.

"What's this?" she asked.

"It's the address you asked for," I replied. A surprised look came across her face. My friend asked me to write the address again in block letters. I was shocked to realize she couldn't read cursive writing.

Many schools have eliminated cursive writing from the curriculum. This worries me. At some time of life, your grandchild will need to sign a document with a legal signature. You don't want your grandchild to sign with kindergarten printing or make a large X. Legal signatures are still necessary in the computer age. Your grandchild's signature is also a symbol of individuality.

According to recent research findings, knowing cursive writing has distinct advantages. Pam Mueller and Daniel Oppenheimer found that students who took handwritten notes were better at answering conceptual questions than students who took notes on laptops.[99] Students who could write legibly seemed to do better academically than those who could not.

Help your grandchild practice cursive writing. The day will come when she or he will thank you for it.

This chapter has given you a range of ideas for at-home activities to share with your grandchild: cursive writing practice, art as personal expression, fostering a grandchild's interests, cooking together, successful sleepovers, and reading aloud. The next chapter focuses on outdoor activities. Open the door, head out, and explore with your grandchild!

---

99 "Why Cursive?" Cursive Logic.

CHAPTER 9

Out-and-About Activities for Grandkids

Walking and Fitness
Going to the Park or Health Club
Magical Museums
Day Trips and Longer Trips
Grandkids' Camp
National Grandparents Day

Now that you have ideas for playing inside with your grandchild, let's discuss some activities that will get you both out of the house. Many of these activities, like going for a walk or visiting a museum, promote lifelong healthy habits. Activities keep you moving and that's good for your health. Let's get going!

Walking and Fitness

Walking is an easy, inexpensive activity to do with your grandchild. The two of you, or more, could start a walking club. Choose a name for your club—The Adventurers, Walking Champs, Two by Two, Determined Duo, Buddies Forever, Walkers and Talkers. Whatever works for you. Decide what the club rules will be, such as walking two blocks or half mile each time you get together. Vary your walking route. Walk outside or, on rainy days, inside at the local mall.

Get a little notebook for you and your grandchild. Use the notebook to keep a walking log and note the date, weather, and distance you walked. Add any comments you wish to make, such as "so windy today."

Always wear comfortable shoes and dress for the weather. Buy inexpensive pedometers with a clip or lanyard for you and your grandchild. Theme walks are fun for grandkids and the whole family. Take a color walk and look for things that are your grandchild's favorite color. Count the number of different birds you see. You could also have a discussion topic for your walk, such as what makes a good friend.

Fitness expert, educator, and author Brett Kilka tells why children need to keep moving in his article, "Top 10 Reasons Children Should Exercise."[100] He shares some shocking numbers. According to the Centers for Disease Control and Prevention (CDC), approximately one third of American children between the ages of ten and seventeen are overweight or obese. Fewer than 25 percent of American children get the recommended sixty minutes of moderate physical activity per day. So many American children are overweight that some experts think this will be the first generation not to outlive their parents.

Kilka says greater rates of physical activity are associated with children's higher reading and math scores.

Physical activity helps brain development.

Being active in childhood tends to carry over into adulthood. And physical activity helps to reduce anxiety and depression. From my child development training, I know physical activity, such as playing catch, improves eye-hand coordination. Kilka

---

100 Brett Kilka, "Top 10 Reasons Children Should Exercise," Act Fitness.

thinks physical activity for children is more important than ever. Don't let your grandchild become a couch potato.

Sally Wendkos Olds writes about jogging with her grandson when he was eight years old and she was fifty-seven.[101] In in her book *Super Granny*, she tells how this stayed in her grandson's mind, and he continued to jog as an adult. One of the highlights of Old's life was jogging in Central Park on New Year's Eve. At midnight, Olds and her grandson joined the jogging throng, stopping a few times for the champagne served along the route. "Every time I wear the T-shirt we received that night, I treasure the memory of that special experience," she writes.

You may share other sports with your grandchild, such as tennis, swimming, horseback riding, skiing, whatever it may be. Maybe you could take golf lessons and practice together. Miniature golf is also fun to play.

Going to a Park or Health Club

Many parents don't let their children play outside because of safety concerns. This is understandable. You may live in a high-traffic area. Crosswalks may not be clearly marked. If playing outside or going for a walk is difficult in your area or where your grandchild lives, take your grandchild to a local park, or a gym, health club, or YMCA. More than 22 percent of health clubs are offering programs for children.[102] Health clubs have more than 4.8 million members under age eighteen and 1.13 million between six and twelve years of age, according to industry experts. One club, The Little Gym in Scottsdale,

101 Sally Wendkos Olds, *Super Granny: Great Stuff to Do with Your Grandkids* (New York: Sterling Publishing Co., Inc., 2009), 193-194
102 "Health Clubs for Children are a Growing Trend," Club Industry.

Arizona, serves children as young as four months old and up to twelve years old.

Many health / fitness clubs offer special activities for children. Before you go to a health club or gym, check age requirements, the fee scale, extra fees, and supervision of children. Also ask about the adult-to-child ratio.

Another concept, a mobile gym, which operates on a franchise basis, markets to daycare facilities and preschools. Contact the business bureau in your town to see if any of these clubs are available.

Unless you're attacked by mosquitoes or have hay fever, going to the park is always fun. The GransNet website explores the park idea in a website article, "Taking Your Grandchildren to the Park."[103] City-dwelling grandkids will love the chance to expend energy and run in an open space. Hide-and-seek is always fun for children. Watch your grandchild closely, however, and keep her or him within sight. While it's worth it to bring a football, the article notes, your grandchild will likely want you to join the game.

The playground is the main attraction of any park. Bring a towel with you if it has rained recently and use it to dry the slide. You can push your grandchild's swing or swing yourself. My sister-in-law had an excellent suggestion for keeping track of children. Before the family went on a trip, she bought her three children the ugliest caps she could find. The caps had giant dots on them and were easy to spot in a crowd. If a child wandered away, she would look for the ugliest caps. Wearing a cap also shields your grandchild from the sun.

---

103 "Taking Your Grandchild to the Park," GransNet.

Magical Museums

Visiting museums is another thing to do with your grandchild. Metropolitan areas have more museums than smaller cities and towns. Museums are magical.

Before you head out, check the museum hours, admission fees, and parking situation. Review the museum rules and make sure your grandchild understands them. You don't want the visit to be like the viral Facebook video in which a five-year old knocks over sculpture. His parents counter the bill they receive with the idea that the sculpture should have been displayed more securely. Talk to your grandchildren about museum behavior and museum rules. These are the rules I suggest.

- No eating in the museum, unless you decide to eat in the restaurant. Your grandchild can't eat candy or chew gum or munch on a cookie.
- A museum is a walking place, not a running place. Chasing others and playing tag is for outside.
- Unless this is a participation museum, there is no climbing or sitting on anything. Your grandchild may sit on museum benches and cafeteria chairs.
- Use an inside voice when you're at the museum. A soft voice, even a whisper, is best in the museum.
- To avoid collisions with people or artifacts, a grandchild should turn off their cell phone. There will be no texting while at the museum.
- Be aware of tours and tour guides and let them go by. Watch where you're going and don't wander away with a tour group.

Rochester has a branch of the Minnesota Children's Museum. One exhibit, "Framed: Step into Art," ran from June 2018 through September 2018. The exhibit had three dimensional paintings that seemed to leap off the canvas. Kids could go inside the 3D paintings and become part of the artwork. After touring the exhibits, visitors created their own artwork. "This exhibit fosters the development of creative and critical thinking, collaboration and communication skills through the visual arts," according to the museum website.

Another exhibit, "Can You Power Up the City?", courtesy of Rochester Public Utilities, lets visitors generate electrical power by hand. Find out if there is a children's museum in your town or nearby town by searching online or asking a librarian at the local library.

Day Trips and Longer Trips

Day trips are something else to do with a grandchild. Rochester is in the southeastern part of Minnesota. Although the city is growing, the Twin Cities is larger, and grandmas take their grandkids there for the day. They may go shopping, see a play, attend a dog show, or tromp through the Mall of America. Having a day with your grandchild is fun and gives parents a day off. If you're planning a day trip, be sure to bring along any medicine your grandchild takes. Bring water in a reusable bottle. If you're going to be outside on a summer day, bring sunscreen. Make sure your cell phone is charged in case of emergency.

Joining a Road Scholar program may be an activity you would like to research. I logged into the website and found trips about exploring the Northwoods, rafting in the Grand Canyon, learning about wolves, becoming a crime scene investigator, learning about Southwestern archaeology, jewelry making, learning magic tricks, sailing, and going on overseas trips. Prices range from $799 to $4,895 or more for overseas trips. The activity level for each trip is noted in a bar graph.

Click on a specific tour to understand the pricing system. Road Scholar requires a travel deposit, which ranges from $100 to $500. The tour description tells you the number of days, cost of an adult's trip, cost of a child's trip, tells which meals are covered, whether the package includes lectures, field trips, hands-on experiences, a group leader, the "assurance plan." These are group trips, and you have the support of being with a group and socializing with members. Admittedly, some trips are costly, others are reasonably priced.

Bring legal documents when you're on a trip. Your grandchild may need identification, a passport, and in our case when we took the twins to Alaska, a letter of permission from their father, who was still alive then. This recommendation came from our travel agent, and we followed it. Before we left for the Alaskan cruise and land trip, I assembled a packet for each twin that contained the itinerary, meal vouchers on the ship, and information about Alaska. Each twin was responsible for their own packet.

Bring your grandchild's medications with you. The medications should be in their original bottles, not pill cases or plastic zipper bags. Customs agents need to see the prescribing physician's name, prescription number, and date of medication. Check the expiration dates on all medications. Dispose of outdated medications properly. The public health department can give you instructions on safe disposal.

Safety comes first when traveling with a grandchild.

Grandkids' Camp

If a prize were to be given for the best grandparent-grandchild idea, I think it goes to my sister and brother-in-law. Ever since their five grandchildren were little, they hosted a Cousins' Camp at their cabin in Wisconsin.

Cousins' Camp started with two grandchildren spending a few days with their grandparents. It grew as the number of grandchildren grew. Cousins' Camp had three goals: get to know their grandkids, help grandkids know each other, and give grandkids reasons to remember their grandparents. There were two basic rules: a grandchild had to be four years old to attend camp, and no parents were allowed.

I emailed my sister-in-law and asked for more information. Her reply was touching and funny. She said the activities changed as the grandchildren got older. Early on, there was usually one craft activity and back-up activities in case of rain. If my memory is correct, she managed to get grandsons to do needlework, and they enjoyed it. Swimming in the lake (life jackets for the younger ones) was a daily activity. Reading aloud was another activity, and the first book she read was *Paddle-to-the-Sea* by Holling C. Holling, a true classic.

Meals were simple—tacos, hot dogs, hamburgers, summer fruit, and cookies. Hiking in the woods was a regular activity, and so were contests. There was a fishing contest (a family favorite) and an outdoor cherry pit spit contest. Prizes were awarded for the longest spit, shortest spit, and juiciest spit. Every evening ended with a rousing Bingo game, my sister-in-law recalled, with cheers from a rowdy grandpa. Later, when the grandkids became teenagers, they went on adventure hikes.

The hikes were several miles long. Grandkids followed clues, learned how to use a compass, and learned nature facts.

Some hikes had themes associated with books. One theme was to rescue the princess, a worn doll, from the castle, a house made of twigs. On long hikes, grandpa followed in the Ranger in case a grandchild became tired or injured. The culmination of the hike was canoeing across the narrowest part of the lake *without* paddles, only hands.

Cousins' Camp taught the grandkids to cooperate and help younger ones and today, they still talk about the wonderful times they had together.

When two granddaughters cleaned out their rooms in preparation for moving, they found some of the things they made at Cousin's Camp. "They will never forget the adventure hike where they had to wade through a foot of muck," my sister-in-law wrote. If she puts out a bowl of cherries, the grandkids start practicing their spits. After all, it's a family tradition. You may create your own version of Cousins' Camp. It doesn't have to be elaborate, just age-appropriate, well planned, and loving.

National Grandparents Day

Your grandchild will be enthusiastic if you attend National Grandparents Day at their school. While this isn't a public holiday, schools across the country celebrate it to bring generations together. Grandparents and grandchildren join in shared activities: story-telling, make a greeting card, poster making, sing-alongs, and reading poetry.

Susan V. Bosak writes about National Grandparents Day in "Grandparents Day Planning & Activity Guide."[104] There has been a demographic shift in America, she begins, and it created connections for recent generations and connections for

104 Susan V. Bosak, "Grandparents Day Planning & Activity Guide," The Legacy Project.

multiple generations. The generations include yours, the three generations before yours: parents, grandparents, and great grandparents.

Bosak thinks schools need to give children a chance to show the love they have for grandparents and grandparents need to show the love they have for grandchildren. This helps to create new memories, validate older adults, let grandparents share experiences, and foster community relations. You get to see your grandchild in a school setting. Bringing generations together is the sum of the past, present, and future. National Grandparents Day is always the first Sunday in September following Labor Day. Circle it on your calendar now.

Grandma-grandchild activities create precious memories. As your grandchild ages, these experiences become more precious. Author Sally Wendkos Olds has five grandchildren and writes about spending individual time with them. "It's as if I know what I'm supposed to do: I'm carrying on an ancient tradition of grandmothering and child care, and I'm totally at peace with the world and myself."

West Chester University, part of the University of Pennsylvania, has a unique idea for grandmothers and grandchildren—help them learn together.[105] For some participants, the program was a chance to remember college days. Other participants were visiting a university campus for the first time. The three-day program happens once a summer and includes staying in a dorm, eating in the dining hall, playing and learning side by side, entertainment, and learning about specific topics. The topics were eclectic: producing and anchoring family newscasts, DNA, astronomy, virtual reality public speaking, and tai chi.

---

105 Bill Rettew, "Grandparents and Grandchildren Learn Together at WCU," *The Mercury*.

Out-and-about activities connect you with the community, nearby communities, and your grandchild. Getting out is also good for your health. Shared activities are special times for both of you. Years from now, when your grandchild is grown, you will remember these activities, smile to yourself, and say, "I'm so glad we did that."

CHAPTER 10

Relationships Change with Time

Physical Growth
Emotional Growth
Service Learning
Supporting a Grandchild's Dreams
Adult-to-Adult Relationship

If you asked me to summarize this chapter with one word, I would say "adaptation." The relationship between you and your grandchild will shift as your grandchild matures. I started to notice changes when the twins came home for college breaks. Their conversation was more mature, their goals were more defined, and they were more independent. To me, it seemed as if the twins had changed from teens to adults overnight.

Watching the twins mature was a happy experience for the most part. Then, without any warning, I would go backward in time and feel sad. Happy and sad are strong, opposing feelings, and feeling them together made me uncomfortable.

Grandmas need to be aware of the changes
that happen to relationships over time.

Physical Growth

One morning my granddaughter walked into the kitchen for breakfast. Her appearance startled me because she looked so much like her mother. Her face was similar, her hair and eyes were brown, and her expressions were the same. She even walked like Helen. For a second or two, it seemed like Helen was alive again. "Don't cry," I told myself. "Don't cry." I managed to keep my feelings under control. Later, I mentioned this experience to John.

"She looks more like Helen every day," he said, and shook his head in wonderment.

"I know," I said.

Our grandson looks a bit like his mother, but not as much as his sister. Although the twins' similarities to their mother give me occasional twinges of grief, I usually feel joy. I'm not alone. Audrey Mettel shares similar feelings in a *Catholic Herald* website article.[106] She thinks the best years are watching grandchildren grow into responsible adults. As she writes, "Every loss that aging brings, whether physical or emotional, is offset by the addition of another measure of joy from my offspring."

While the twins aren't tall adults, they are strong. In high school, my granddaughter was on the gymnastics team, and she is still strong and agile. My grandson was briefly on the track team and stays fit by going to a health club. I appreciated their physical strength when the time came to move out of our three-level home to a wheelchair-friendly townhome. John and I had moved many times, only this time I was doing it myself. I dreaded the move because we had so much stuff.

The twins helped me dispose of things and helped me move.

106 Audrey Mettel, "The Joy of Watching Grandchildren Grow into Adults," *Catholic Herald*.

To save money, I moved all the kitchen items—dishes, silverware, cooking tools, pots, pans, placemats, and tablecloths—and they moved the big items. The twins, along with my granddaughter's fiancé, moved the couch, easy chairs, dining room table, and dining room chairs. They loaded these things into the back of a truck and carried them into the townhome.

I was amazed when my granddaughter picked up a rolled, ten-by-twelve-foot area rug, carried it to the center of the room, and flipped it open like a genie unrolling a magic carpet. Her feat was magical because the rug landed precisely where I wanted it. The twins' kindness and strength saved us hundreds of dollars.

A grandchild can shoot up in height like a weed. This may have happened to your grandchild. She or he went from being short to being tall in one summer. One of my friends was surprised at her grandson's growth. "He is only twelve years old and he's already two inches taller than I am," she explained. "I wonder how tall he will be when he is an adult."

You may want to keep a diary or record of the physical changes you see in your grandchild. The diary for an infant may include crawling, attempts to stand, the day your grandchild stood up, and when your grandchild started walking. These are true achievements and worth noting. You may want to keep a height chart on a wall. The diary for a teenage granddaughter may include notes and photos of ballet lessons, a dance recital, and the recital program.

Emotional Growth

Physical and emotional growth often progress at different rates. Maturity takes time to develop. You may see glimpses of it when your grandchild is younger, and then see steady progress a year or so later. I think the twins' emotional growth was faster than their peers' growth. The death of both parents can do that to a child—or an adult, for that matter. Fast emotional growth does not mean it was easy. On the contrary, it was difficult for all of us.

Emotional growth draws you closer to your grandchild. Infants need to feel loved, safe, and understood. Older children need to feel these things as well and want to be valued and trusted. Meri Wallace, a licensed social worker, describes children's emotional needs in her article, "Understanding Children's Emotional Needs."[107] She makes an important point at the beginning of the article. "As children grow, they continue to need their parent's love and attention." Similarly,

> children continue to need their
> grandma's love and attention.

In a child's mind (and grandchild's mind) time equals attention and attention adds up to love. Wallace illustrates the point this way: time = attention = love. You can foster your grandchild's emotional growth by spending time with them.

Loving gestures—a smile, hug, or pat on the back—also promote emotional growth. In my experience, a teenage grandchild may resist a hug. Before you give them a hug it may be wise to ask for their permission. Say "I love you often" to reassure your grandchild.

Every grandchild, no matter how old they are, needs to be respected. Acknowledging their opinions, feelings, and desires is important. Your grandchild may try out for the tennis team and not make it. You may think acknowledging their effort will

---

107 Meri Wallace, "Understanding Children's Emotional Needs," Psychology Today.

make them feel bad, but they will feel worse if you ignore what happened. Saying something like "I know you're disappointed, but you can be proud of setting an ambitious goal" will help them feel encouraged to keep trying.

Grandkids need to be praised and members of the Grandma Force can do this. Congratulate your grandchild on being selected for a leading role, winning a contest, and other achievements. This leads to the last point in the article—encouragement. Say something reassuring, such as "Don't worry. You'll do better next time." Encouraging words help to protect a child's self-esteem, according to Wallace.

The twins' emotional maturity was evident in daily conversation, in the plans they made, and in their career choices. Emotional maturity and emotional intelligence aren't the same, though the terms are often used interchangeably. This can cause confusion.[108] Emotional maturity is a level of maturity that comes with life experience. Emotional intelligence is the understanding of emotions.

> Having emotional maturity doesn't
> mean one has emotional intelligence.

In his book *Emotional Intelligence: Why It Can Matter More Than IQ*, author Daniel Goleman says human emotions are alerted to protect humans from danger.[109] Goleman contrasts the rational mind and the emotional mind and says they "operate in tight harmony for the most part, intertwining their very different ways of knowing to guide us through the world." The

---

108 Peter Vajda, "Emotional Intelligence or Emotional Maturity?" Management Issues.
109 Daniel Goleman. *Emotional Intelligence: Why It Can Matter More Than IQ* (New York: Bantam Books, 1997), 4, 9.

twins' emotional maturity helped guide me when I became John's primary caregiver.

Elizabeth Fishel and Dr. Jeffrey Jensen Arnett share practical tips for coping with change in their article "Parenting Adult Children: Are You a Good Friend to Your Grown Up Kid?"[110]

They think emerging adults (your grandchild) need a different kind of closeness than when they were younger. Five strategies will help you fine-tune your relationship with a grandchild who is twenty years old or older.

Emerging adults use privacy as a boundary, the authors explain, and you need to respect boundaries. Your grandchild may start to pull away from you and avoid long conversations, for example. Don't take this as a personal affront; it's part of maturing. Even if you're a great conversationalist, listen more than you talk.

Keep doing the things you like to do with your grandchild. You may spend less time with your grandchild, but this makes the time you do spend together more special. Allow more time for planning if you're busy with work and community efforts.

Think about your grandchild's emotional maturity and whether she or he is aware of their feelings. You can help your grandchild stay in touch with their feelings. Naming feelings was discussed in Chapter 6, and you may continue to do this. Perhaps a friend hurt your grandchild's feelings, and your grandchild felt down for days. Acknowledge your grandchild's feelings and offer an alternative, such as, "You don't have to give that person that much power. You're in charge of you."

---

110 Elizabeth Fishel and Jeffrey Jensen Arnett, "Parenting Adult Children: Are You a Good Friend to Your Grown-Up Kid?" AARP.

Service Learning

Service projects are a way for your grandchild to learn about caring. In the process, she or he will learn lessons for a lifetime. Some educators call this *service learning*. Check out the projects in your community. Figure out which ones suit your grandchild best.

"12 Service Projects for Kids," an article on the Points of Light website, divides service projects into younger and older children.[111] Ideas for younger kids include writing letters to enclose in packages for soldiers, contributing to a food drive, filling children's backpacks, and donating gently used clothing to others. Older kids may provide free lawn care or sell hot cider at school (with the school's permission) and donate the proceeds to the charity of their choice. Books and lightly used DVDs may be donated to the public library. Visit residents at a local nursing home and sing carols for them at holiday time. Collect gently used towels, wash and fold them, and donate them to a local charity. Assemble personal hygiene kits (tooth brush, toothpaste, deodorant, comb, shampoo, conditioner) in large plastic zipper bags and donate them to the women's shelter.

Teaching grandchildren to think of others is important. The habits children develop in childhood stick with them into adulthood, the article explains. As soon as you and your grandchild have finished one project, start thinking about the next one. This helps to keep your grandchild interested in service projects. My grandson volunteered for Habitat for Humanity when he was in high school, and he's always willing to help others.

---

111 "12 Service Project Ideas for Kids," Points of Light.

Some service learning ideas are more involved, such as starting a Little Mini Library. The idea started in Hudson, Wisconsin, in 2009 and spread across America quickly. "Take a book, leave a book" was the basis of the idea. I wrote an article about a Mini Library for a local magazine. In preparation for the article, I attended the opening ceremony for the library. Like most of these libraries, it was made of wood, only this one looked like a space ship. A representative of the Rochester Public Library attended the ceremony. "I've seen lots of Little Mini Libraries, but I've never seen one like this!" he exclaimed.

The family welcomed neighbors, unveiled the library, and passed out lemonade and cookies. Creating a Little Mini Library is a gift for the community. You and your grandchild may create the library on your own or with help. Decide where the library will stand, such as in your yard or between yards. Tips from the *Milwaukee Journal Sentinel*'s article "10 Things to Know Before Building Your Little Free Library" will make the project easier.[112]

Doing your research is the first tip. This may include driving around neighborhoods to look at sample libraries. Which one is the best? What makes it the best? You can see photos of these libraries on Pinterest. Some look like ordinary houses, others look like bird houses. There's even one that looks like an illustration from a Dr. Seuss book. Check out other websites too, because some have free construction plans.

Keep the construction simple. Choose a plan that doesn't require carpentry skills or high-tech tools that you don't have or know how to use. Personalize your Little Mini Library. The rocket ship idea was very personal. Your grandchild may paint the box that holds the books, paint the pole, decorate the library with flowers, or stock it with books. Some owners build libraries

112 Ellen Kobe, "10 Things to Know Before Building Your Little Free Library," *Milwaukee Journal Sentinel*.

that match their houses. Building costs add up quickly, so keep all your receipts, and try to stick to your budget.

Because the library is accessible at all hours, you may wish to put a circle of solar lights around the library (the kind that you stick in grass). One homeowner installed a monitor that lets him know every time the door of the library is opened. This grandma-grandchild project could become a meaningful memory. Take a photo of you and your grandchild by the Little Mini Library. Frame the photo and give it to your grandchild.

Edna Rienzi details more service projects in her article, "Helping Your Kids Give Back: 11 Fun Holiday Service Ideas for You and Your Family."[113] The article begins with information from the Wharton School of Business at the University of Pennsylvania. The school learned that people who volunteered to help others a small amount of time felt more efficient and competent. "These feelings gave people the sense that they could do quite a bit with their limited time," according to the article.

A grandchild who has outgrown toys will be glad to give them to a younger child. Outgrown clothing may be donated to The Salvation Army or Goodwill. Get two large boxes. Write "Toys" on one and "Clothes" on the other. Your grandchild may decorate the boxes before you start filling them. Toys and clothing may also be donated to your church rummage sale. You may also pass these things on to a younger relative.

Making greeting cards is an easy, meaningful idea. Sick children will be eager to receive "happy mail," Reinzi notes, and you may deliver cards to a local hospital. Check with a supervisor beforehand. Adopting a soldier is another idea

---

113 Edna Reinzi, "Helping Your Kid Give Back: 11 Fun Holiday Service Ideas for You and Your Family," New Dream.

and can change a life. You can learn more about it by going to http://www.adoptaussoldier.org.

Reinzi purchased ornaments with the St. Jude's logo on them and gave the ornaments to family members for Christmas. Her mother cried when she received her ornament. Search the Internet for organizations that sell items to finance their cause. The Salvation Army has holiday toy drives and always needs donations, especially for pre-teens and teens. Toys for Tots is another organization to check. The last idea is to make fleece blankets for the homeless. The Women's Shelter may also welcome blankets.

As with most things in life, quality over quantity makes a difference in service. Doing service with your grandchild will benefit them for their entire life.

Supporting a Grandchild's Dreams

I think a grandma needs to be aware of their grandchild's dreams and try to make them come true. This can be difficult because a grandchild's dreams may shift often as they grow, but if you show an interest in helping them, they will always be encouraged to follow their interests. Supporting a grandchild's dreams becomes more important the older he or she gets.

My grandson and his high school buddies wanted to build a raft and float down the Zumbro River to the Mississippi. The idea worried me because I didn't know anything about the Zumbro, the water level, launch area, or if there were rocks and rapids. If other parents were worried, they didn't tell me. Fortunately, the boys had some boating experience.

One couple offered to let the boys build the raft in their garage and use their tools. Their generous offer was too good to pass up, and the boys started collecting large plastic milk containers to keep their raft afloat. The boys worked on the raft for weeks and it became more complex, with an upper level and plastic slide going down to the water. The finished raft was so impressive that the father called the local newspaper. A photographer was sent out to photograph the launch.

The article, a Huckleberry Finn kind of story, appeared on the front page of the newspaper. I hadn't seen the raft before and, to me, it resembled a houseboat more than a raft. In the photo, my grandson is standing on the top level of the raft, looking down at the water. Building the raft was a bonding experience for the boys, and they are still friends. My grandson saved the article, a memory of his teenage years and the friends he made.

Because John and I were the twins' guardians, we didn't have to check with their parents before our grandson got involved in the raft project. Before you get involved in a large project with your grandchild, like building a lemonade stand or putting a kayak kit together, consult with the parents. The parents may or may not like your idea.

Now my grandson's dream is to become a medical doctor. In the process, he must decide what his specialty might be. While we encourage conversation about this, we don't interfere but do remain supportive. My granddaughter's photography business continues to grow. She and her husband are also raising foster children. They have been approved by Minnesota Foster, part of the Minnesota Department of Human Services, gone through training, and had five foster children to date. We've met every foster child and welcomed them into our home.

Adult-to-Adult Relationship

By the time they were in their mid-twenties, the twins' roles had changed, and my role had changed. Instead of me encouraging the twins, they encouraged me after John's aorta dissected and during his three operations. They visited John in the Intensive Care Unit (ICU) of the hospital. My granddaughter took photos of Christmas dinner and compiled a slide show for John to see in the ICU. Having an adult relationship with a grandchild is a joy and a blessing.

After the twins received their college degrees, they headed out into the world and went in different directions. My granddaughter had a rewarding job with The Salvation Army headquarters in St. Paul. Her independent photography business was growing, and she started to specialize in wedding photography. My grandson worked in a Mayo Clinic laboratory until he was accepted at The Mayo Clinic School of Medicine. Proud as I was of their accomplishments, I felt lost and unnecessary. Were my grandparenting days over?

The answer turned out to be no. The twins occasionally ask me for advice. When we're together, it's on an adult-to-adult basis. Conversation ranges from current events, to developments in medicine, to hiking in the Grand Canyon, to photography, to appreciating nature, to Midwestern birds and bird watching. Though we don't see each other often, we get together for dinner when we can and stay in touch with email.

I've asked the twins for their opinions and help, particularly my grandson, the medical student. He understands my life as John's primary caregiver. My grandson listens attentively and offers suggestions and help. When I had a racing heartbeat, he checked it with a stethoscope, checked my neck, and announced, "I have to take you to the hospital." He drove me there, stayed with me during intake, and sat with me as tests were done. He left a few hours later to take care of John and stayed with him during the night.

This is just one example of our adult-to-adult relationship. I have the same relationship with my granddaughter and usually follow her advice. My adult-to-adult relationship with the twins is reinforced with words and deeds. You may be at this stage of life and savor it as I do. Tears come to my eyes when people tell me the twins are fine, outstanding adults. Because the twins' story is so inspiring, one of my friends carries their high school graduation photo in her wallet.

Like fine wine, the grandma-grandchild relationship keeps getting better. To make life better for all families and grandkids, you may opt for the proactive route. Much to my surprise, as a grandmother I became an activist and advocate, the subject of the next chapter. The proactive route may also be the route for you.

CHAPTER 11

Becoming an Activist and Advocate

Taking the Proactive Route
Examples of Activism
Working with Organizations
Advocacy
Let's Be Civil
The Grandmother Project
Persistence and Professionalism Count

Grandmas can have a big impact on their families, communities, and the world. Thousands of courageous grandmas are blazing new trails and making wrong things right. Newspapers, magazines, and television programs are filled with stories about these activists. While the stories are interesting to read, members of the Grandma Force can go beyond reading and be proactive. This chapter is filled with ideas of how you can make a difference in the life of your grandchild, your family, and your community.

Taking the Proactive Route

Grandmas need to be agents for change.

Change doesn't happen by itself and, just like lighting a fire, needs a spark. You and I can be the sparks—people who transform ideas into reality. Until we moved to a small Midwestern town, I didn't realize I was an activist. I was a new member of the American Association of University Women (AAUW) at the time, and the leadership asked for project suggestions.

I knew the public library didn't have a story hour, and suggested AAUW start and staff weekly story times for the community. AAUW members liked the idea and several immediately volunteered to read. Before we launched the project, I went to the library and talked with the head librarian. I explained AAUW involvement and volunteer staffing and promised to recruit readers and read often myself. "After story hour, the kids could look at library books," I concluded. For several long seconds there was silence in the room.

Instead of the smile I anticipated, the librarian looked upset. "That would disturb the books," she countered. I was so shocked I was almost speechless.

Disturbing books was the purpose of a public library. In hindsight, I think she might have been overworked, underpaid, and weary of cataloging books. Story hour kids would mess up her neat Dewey Decimal System rows. I thanked the librarian for her time and asked her to think about the idea.

The next week I contacted the librarian and asked to meet with her again. She agreed and, after some discussion, approved the story hour idea. Children signed up for the story hour ahead of time. I made a smiley face nametag for each child. I read at the first story hour and it went well. Succeeding story hours also went well. We moved away a few years later, so I don't know if the story hours continued. At least I launched the program and helped the community.

If you feel strongly about an issue, you may wish to form an activist group. Post an announcement on a grandmothers' blog and see what happens. Does your idea garner any interest? Be aware that starting and sustaining a group is a massive undertaking, and you need to be prepared for this. The concept may require more financing than you originally thought. As time passes, your enthusiasm may dwindle.

Writing a petition and getting others to sign it may be something else you're willing to tackle. Fortunately, you don't have to knock on doors to get signatures. An email blast can generate hundreds of signatures in minutes.

Don't let a few obstacles or setbacks get you down. If you believe in your idea, pursue it with all your might. You need to stay focused on your original concept and check on things regularly. One grandma's idea can ripple out into the community, as the following examples indicate.

Examples of Activism

Many grandmas have become activists.

At eighty-nine years of age, Pearl Malkin started her own business called Happy Canes, in which she decorated walking sticks with artificial flowers.[114] She set a goal of making $3,500 in venture capital. Malkin believed in her product, and she had a plan. Her first purchase was a wire cutter to snip flower stems. She also planned to stock up on artificial flowers. This energetic, gutsy grandma thought she could make ten to twenty canes a day. Malkin wasn't merely a grandma with a goal, she was a woman of determination and vision.

---

114 Parija Kavilanz, "89-Year-Old Grandma Hits Kickstarter Goal," CNN.

Some contemporary grandmas decide to finish their schooling. Mildred Walker is one of these people.[115] Walker checked "receive high school diploma" off her bucket list at age seventy-three. Before she received her diploma, Walker worked in a cafeteria and drove a school bus to make ends meet. Now she is thinking about getting more education. Grandmas like Walker believe in education and believe in themselves.

There are thousands of grandmas like Walker and Malkin. Grandmas are competing in marathons, serving on boards, running for office, and starting businesses. Nothing is going to keep these grandmas from their self-appointed tasks. As soon as they reach one goal, these grandmas set new ones.

Some grandmas want to improve communities. Others want to improve the world. While our goals differ, courageous grandmothers are attracting the attention of visual and print media.

The Cape Cod Newsletter, a free online publication, carried a story about Donna Hannigan, a member of the Cape Cod Grandmothers Against Gun Violence.[116] The group's mission is to educate the public about this violence. Everyone is welcome to join the organization, men, women, and people of all political parties. Members aren't opposed to owning guns, they are opposed to gun violence, and focus on two issues—background checks, and making gun trafficking a federal crime.

Photojournalist and grandmother Paola Gianturco is a woman with ambitious goals.[117] The author of *Grandmother Power*, she wants to publicize what grandmothers are doing

---

115 Kristen Keller, "73-Year-Old Grandmother Completes Her GED," *Jersey Journal*.

116 "Grandmothers Against Gun Violence Expand Mission," *Cape Cod newsletter*.

117 Paola Gianturco, *Grandmother Power: A Global Phenomenon* (Brooklyn, NY: Powerhouse Books, 2012), 8.

about HIV / AIDS, preserving culture, the environment, human rights, education, justice, spiritual life, health, politics, and energy. Gianturco says this is the first time the grandmothers of the world have campaigned for political and social change. "As a grandmother myself, I suspect this activism is stimulated by our tightly connected, troubled world, which impels us to improve the future for our grandchildren."

Katie Harris, founder of the Nana Café in East London, England, is an example. The café has become a destination with a difference, according to *The Guardian* reporter Helena Drakakis.[118] Harris created a combination café and craft center to combat isolation and depression in women sixty years old and older. The idea was inspired by the entrepreneur's eighty-eight-year-old grandmother. The idea sounds cheesy, Harris admits, yet it is bringing women together.

"I never understood why older people are separated in society or abandoned, and the café breaks down those barriers," she is quoted as saying.

Working at the café has given older women new purpose. One woman is grateful she can meet people and share her skills. Another woman said working at the café was challenging and rewarding. The work isn't about money, it's about giving back and helping others. The older women who staff the café prepare tasty food, sell it at affordable prices, and get involved with patrons. Because of its food (which apparently is darned good) and its atmosphere, the Nana Café is a favorite for many Londoners. The nanas don't get upset at nursing mothers or screaming children because they've seen it all and know how to help. This is a café with heart.

Carolyn Jackson of New Haven, Connecticut, fifty-five

118 Helena Krakakis, "Nana Café Embraces the Talents of Grandmothers," *The Guardian*.

years old, founded Grandparents On the Move, a support program for caregivers.[119] Because she raised her own three grandchildren, Jackson knew the challenges of caregiving all too well. Grandparents on the Move addresses the financial, legal, and educational needs of grandparents. Gathering funds to create the organization took years. Jackson managed to do it and took grandparents to a conference in Washington, DC.

Brigette Castellano, sixty-six years old, is co-founder of the National Committee of Grandparents for Children's Rights in Albany, New York.[120] Castellano's daughter was killed by a drunk driver in 1995. At the time, Castellano's daughter and grandson were living with her, but the child's father went to court, and he obtained custody of his daughter. Despite this heartbreak, Castellano contacted other grandparents in the same situation, and they worked to pass the New York State Grandparent Caregiver Rights Act. This legislation says the court must consider grandparents in custody disputes.

Brigette Castellano, Carolyn Jackson, and Katie Harris are activists fighting to write wrongs they experienced. You can be one, too.

Working with Organizations

Working with an existing organization
may be easier and more effective than
creating your own group.

There are many organizations that combat many societal ills, or work to improve communities. One example is a Cana-

---

119 Amy Goyer, "Grandparents in Action," AARP.
120 Goyer, "Grandparents in Action," AARP.

dian organization, the Grandmother Advocacy Network (GRAN), which works to improve the lives of grandmothers and vulnerable children in sub-Saharan Africa. It's a non-partisan group and, according to the GRAN website, members educate, advocate, and partner with other groups. Currently, GRAN is working with the United Nations on the sustainable development of health, education, and gender equality.

AARP has many volunteer opportunities. Changing communities for older adults is a cause that may interest you. *Where We Live: Communities for All Ages*, by Nancy LeaMond, AARP Executive Vice President of Community, State and National Affairs, focuses on housing needs.[121] She describes the chapters as "calls to action." Your action may include coming up with an innovative housing idea, exploring your community, and completing an online AARP survey.

AARP recommends building houses for all ages calls for the return of "middle housing," affordable homes in the right location. Too often, however, older adults find this housing doesn't exist. Tiny homes may be a solution, and although these homes are small, they can be mighty. Neighborhoods of tiny homes are springing up across the country. Neighbors need to be encouraged to help other neighbors, according to the report. Improving transportation, supporting wellness, helping residents feel safe, and sharing spaces are other issues.

I've been a member of the Minnesota Medical Association Alliance (MMAA) for decades. Members of the organization are physicians' or researchers' spouses. The organization is for males and females, and its purpose is to improve community health. I became so concerned about children's health that I wrote a series of activity books for kids in third through fifth

---

121 Nancy LeaMond. *Where We Live: Communities for All Ages* (Washington, DC: AARP, 2018), 7.

grades entitled *Food Label Detective*, *Catching the Exercise Thief*, and *Cracking the Health Words Code*. The Minnesota Medical Association (MMA) gave the Alliance $1,000 to publish the first book, and we printed thousands.

Before I started writing, I researched child nutrition, physical activity, and medical terminology. The activity books were professionally illustrated by Mary McKee, the illustrator for the State of Minnesota. McKee could do anything—sketches, paintings, calligraphy, comics. She chose a comic style for the activity books. Unfortunately, the Alliance didn't have the funds to publish full-color comics like those in the newspaper. The illustrations were line drawings only.

Each page began with a fact, then stated the source of the fact, and was followed by an activity. The activity books were forty-eight pages long, a common page length for this genre. I worked hard on the books and hoped they would be fun for kids.

The MMAA donated thousands of books to area schools. The Duluth, Minnesota branch gave books away at its biannual health fair. A volunteer translated *Food Label Detective* into colloquial Spanish, and we gave these books away too. Books were donated to the Channel One Food Shelf in Rochester because many clients were Hispanic. I also wrote a series of pocket information cards for preteens and teens: "Tobacco Smoke is No Joke!", "Facts on Fizz," and "Meth is Death." Thousands of these cards were given away.

I didn't charge anything for my writing or make any money on these projects. My goal was to improve children's lives. I couldn't have done these things on my own. Having the backing of the Minnesota Medical Association and the MMAA transformed my dreams into reality. You may find similar support in your community. Talk with social services, area churches, branches of national organizations, and service organizations—Kiwanis, Rotary, American Legion, and others. You may be willing to help with an existing project.

Advocacy

Grandmas can be activists and advocates.

What's the difference? The Free Online Dictionary defines an advocate as a person who upholds or defends a cause. This person is a supporter, someone who intercedes on behalf of another. A more technical definition is a person who pleads a case in a court of law. When I think of an advocate, I think of a patient advocate, a role I've had and continue to have.

I acted as my husband's advocate when I drove him to the hospital emergency department. I was his advocate when he had three emergency operations. I was his advocate when he was in intensive care for a month. I was his advocate when he was in a nursing home for eight months. Tasks included making sure John was cared for properly, respectfully, and getting information about his care, Medicare regulations, and health care costs. You may find yourself in a situation that requires advocacy.

For example, your grandchild may be in the hospital. Things seem to be going well, but when you visit your grandchild, you see that she or he is in pain. In a case like this, you may talk to the head of the health care team, usually a physician, or talk to the head nurse. Many hospitals have a patient advocate on staff.

I've been my husband's patient advocate during two surgeries, once when surgeons installed a Dacron descending aorta, and once when the connection between the Dacron and actual aorta failed. Today, I'm still his advocate and the tips I learned may help you. Attending medical rounds is the first tip. The physician in charge of John's health care team invited me to go on morning rounds. I accepted his invitation. My younger daughter, a licensed family therapist, came with me, and the reports we heard were extremely technical. Although I've learned many medical terms during sixty-one years as John's wife, I didn't understand what was going on.

At the end, the supervising physician (who knew John was emeritus staff) asked if I had any questions. "Yes," I answered. "Could you summarize that in English?" The physician simplified his explanation and I thanked him.

John was in the ICU of the hospital for a month. The health care team kept him in an artificial coma to promote healing. John's surgical scar started on his chest, went around his left side, to his back. The health care team referred to the scar as a wound. I called it a trench because it was so deep three ribs were showing. A month later, John's health care team slowly brought him out of the coma. Regaining consciousness took a week.

He was transferred to a nursing home for wound care and stayed eight months. I visited him twice a day and occasionally ate meals with him. The nursing home hired a new social worker, and she looked frazzled. She was one person in a facility that contained hundreds. I could never do her job. Brief conversations with her made me wonder if she had reviewed any of John's paperwork. I met the social worker by the elevator one morning.

"Hi Mrs. Hodgson," she said. "I should talk with you, but I'm too busy." The elevator door opened, and she entered and disappeared. I wished the social worker had talked with me before she ordered psychological testing for John. When I received the bill for the testing—several hundred dollars—I was angry.

John didn't need psychological testing or counseling. He needed to rest, regain his strength, and recover from three operations and ICU psychosis. ICU psychosis is a disorder caused by sensory deprivation, sleep deprivation, being in a strange place, and pain. The patient may become anxious, confused about time and place, and may become violent. John was never violent, but he confused his early medical career with his present career and thought he was back at NASA Houston. I went to the nursing supervisor on John's floor and asked her why psychological testing was ordered.

"The social worker talked with your husband several times," she explained. "He cried every time."

"He has ICU psychosis," I replied. It was the nurse's turn to look perplexed. Maybe she didn't understand the term. Because the nurse looked like she was in a hurry, I didn't explain further. I summarized John's story, said he was recovering from multiple surgeries and being in a coma. "I'm not paying this bill," I declared firmly. "We have thousands and thousands of dollars of medical bills, and I could use that money for groceries."

The nurse was an empathetic, kind, and helpful person. Disagreeing with her made me feel awful. While I try to avoid confrontations, sometimes they are necessary. This was one of those times. I represented John when he couldn't represent himself. Nothing would deter me. The nurse offered to check with the medical center and kept her promise. Another bill arrived from the center and it was for $50. I paid it.

I will always be John's advocate. A situation may arise with your grandchild where you need to be an advocate. Working parents may be unable to attend a conference, need back-up, or need more information on an issue. You can do these things. Indeed, your advocacy helps a child and the family. Grandmother advocacy is needed in certain situations around the world. Advocate, activist, or both, you'll get more done if you're civil to others.

Let's Be Civil

Americans seem to have lost their civility in recent years. They hurl insults, throw rocks, make threats, and harm each other. I saw protestors kick a man repeatedly in the head on television and wondered if the man survived the vicious attack. Seeing violence breaks my heart. Yes, we have the right to demonstrate. Let's do so in a civilized way. I think we need to tamp down the rhetoric, reduce the polarization, and come together as Americans. Unless we do this, we won't have to worry about another government taking over the nation. America will destroy itself.

I long for the simple days of my childhood when people were civil. While some people were grumpy, Americans in general disagreed with one another in measured ways. Then, too, we were at war and came together to defend the nation. Civility is sorely needed. Unfortunately, many people have forgotten what it looks like.

Civility in America began when our nation began. George Washington wrote *Rules of Civility and Decent Behavior in Company and Conversation* when he was sixteen years old. *Foundations* magazine posted an article about the rules on its website.[122] While the rules may sound fussy, or even silly today, they focus on something that seems to have been lost—thinking

122 "George Washington's Rules of Civility & Decent Behavior in Company and Conversation," *Foundations Magazine*.

of others. "These rules proclaim our respect for others and in turn give us the gift of self-respect and heightened self-esteem," the article declares.

There isn't room here for Washington's 110 rules, but I can highlight some of them. Rule twenty-two: "Show not yourself glad at the Misfortune of another though he were your enemy." Rule seventy-three: "Think before you Speak pronounce not imperfectly nor bring out our Words too hastily but orderly & distinctly."

Rule one hundred ten may be the most powerful, "Labor to keep alive in your breast that little spark of celestial fire called conscience." We should all read these rules to remind ourselves of basic manners, kindness, and civility. George Washington's book is available as a free Kindle edition, a paperback, or a hardcover book. I try to follow Washington's rules and my conscience. I'm careful about what I post on social media and don't think websites are places for hateful words.

I met a woman who became my model of civility. When John and I supported a smoke-free restaurant ordinance for Rochester, we were in frequent contact with the public health department as the campaign progressed. I admired the director of the department, an informed, gracious, dedicated woman. Nothing fazed her. She spoke in a calm voice when tempers flared and kept citing facts about the dangers of tobacco use. Facts won. I try to model her behavior and disagree with others calmly and politely. If we work on it, we can disagree with someone, still like them, and have them as a friend.

The Grandmother Project[123]

One of my goals is to change the perception of grandmothers. We're living longer, staying healthier, and engaged with life. Yet some governments and legislators don't see us. Grandmas are invisible. When I was doing the research for this book, I came across The Grandmother Project and Judi Aubel, PhD, MPH, one of its founders. Aubel is president of The Grandmother Project and, if she has her way, grandmothers will be invisible no longer. The grandmothers of the world will be consulted and included and valued.

The Grandmother Project, a non-profit organization, was founded in 2003. The mission of the organization is to validate and strengthen the knowledge, skills, and leadership capacity of grandmothers around the world. Aubel is the author of *Involving Grandmothers to Promote Child Nutrition, Health and Development*. Her guide for program planners and managers has three objectives: 1) explore the relevance of including grandmothers in child development programs; 2) identify programs that have involved grandmothers; 3) recommend ways to increase grandmother involvement in the future.

I downloaded her report and underlined key points—points that inspired me.[124] In the introduction, Aubel says the perception and stereotype of older women as being needy still exists. Another stereotype is that illiterate women are unintelligent and therefore unable to learn. These falsehoods are influenced by ageism—applying negative stereotypes to

---

123 Judi Aubel, "Grandmother Project: Involving Grandmothers to Promote Child Nutrition, Health and Development," report on the Grandmother Project website.

124 You may download the report by going to www.wvi.org/sits/default/files. The report is eighty plus pages long, so be prepared to use lots of paper and ink.

older people—and you may have experienced it.

Ageism isn't fun, as I discovered. I participated in a medical study on heart function. The nurse looked at my health records before she gave me instructions. In a slow, patronizing voice, she told me put my feet on the line on the floor, walk down the hall as fast as I could, turn around at the marker, and return to the starting line. The nurse would time my sprint. "Do you understand the instructions?" she asked.

Yes, I understood her instructions. What I couldn't understand were her agonizingly slow delivery and patronizing voice. Obviously, the nurse thought I was demented. At that moment, I decided not to tell her I was on a walking program. I started off at a good clip, zig-zagged around a physician who darted across the hall, narrowly missed a nurse who suddenly came out of a room, reached the marker, turned around, and raced back, barely out of breath. The nurse was astonished.

"You did well," she said with a surprised look on her face.

While that pleased me, after I left the hospital I was annoyed at myself. Why didn't I say something? I think it's because I don't welcome confrontation. My response would be different today because I'm a different person—a seasoned grandmother. I would say, "You can talk to me in a normal way and normal voice. I don't have dementia." We can't let ageism stop us from doing what needs to be done.

Aubel's guide identified steps that grandmothers could take to improve children's education. These steps come from a review of the literature and include strengthening family systems, building on cultural roles and values, integrating traditional and modern childcare practices, building on community resources/strengths, garnering more support, and building social capital. That's an impressive list. Aubel's conclusion: "There is a significant discrepancy between the policy statements of key international organizations that support the inclusion of grandmothers in child development programs and the virtual absence of these senior women in child development programs."

The analysis and documentation of a grandmother's role in different societies around the world is limited, according to Aubel. Some studies ignore the contributions of grandmothers or give them minimal credit. Grandmothers are givers and the report describes some of their contributions to cultures and nations. Together, grandmothers and grandfathers can do even more, and Aubel has recommendations for grandmothers. I revised the wording to make her recommendations more personal.

One recommendation is to make teachers and students aware of what you and other grandmas do. Another recommendation is to share cultural knowledge and skills. The third recommendation has been discussed previously: support service learning. Make school subjects come alive with stories, songs, and crafts from your culture. Working with local schools helps you develop a true partnership with them. This partnership includes attending programs, conferences, and supporting home study. In short, you need to be a present grandma, not an absent one.

Being John's primary caregiver and work on various writing projects often keeps me from volunteering. I don't have the time or energy to be present. Therefore, I limit my projects and choose ones that mesh with my schedule. Most of the projects I'm involved with let me work from home.

When an organization asked me to serve as co-president, I agreed. The three other co-presidents are younger than I, and working with them may be challenging, something I admitted to a friend. "You are the voice of experience," she said. "You know our history and know what's needed." I had been president of the organization before, and her comment convinced me to volunteer again.

Persistence and Professionalism Count

Persistent grandmas have clear goals, and those goals are often working toward the betterment of their community. Remez Sasson writes about persistence in an article titled "Achieving Success Requires Patience and Persistence."[125] He says big goals take time and patience and those who lack it can develop it. Sasson thinks patience is closely related to self-discipline. When you strengthen your self-discipline you are strengthening your patience. If progress is to be made, you must be patient and do your best. Persistent people are realists. They are prepared for the glitches, barriers, and setbacks they encounter.

One of my goals is to get more wheelchair van parking in Rochester. We have a side-loading van. John needs enough space to roll down the ramp and clear it. There is a sign on the window next to the ramp that says, "Wheelchair accessible vehicle. Please do not park within eight feet." We've seen non-handicapped people park in van spaces. People don't seem to understand that the open space next to the van is for unloading, not parking their cars.

Recently I saw an adjoining space with the words "Do not Park" in the center. This is an excellent idea and I'm going to pursue it—persistently.

A friend of mine worked hard on a grant application. When she finished it, she discovered she had missed the deadline. Groan. Two choices were available to her: ask for an extension

125 Sasson, Remez, "Achieving Success Requires Patience and Persistence," Success Consciousness.

or submit a grant to another organization. She chose the second option.

Persistent grandmas keep going, review the steps they have taken, and change course if necessary. You don't have to be a lonely activist or advocate. Ask for help. You'll feel better if you do. We can make a difference when we work together.

The last few years I've worked with young people in management positions. They don't seem to have the skill sets for their positions. Emails aren't answered. Phone calls aren't returned. Reminders aren't sent. I spoke for free at one event and had spent hours on my presentation. The manager never greeted me or thanked me. If we're going to change communities, we need to be organized, courteous, and professional. Most important, we need to learn how to work with younger people.

Sometimes I'm the one who sends an email reminder. "I'm looking forward to seeing you on September 1st at 2 p.m. when I talk about Creating the Happiness You Seek." I also send information emails. "I'll need a microphone, podium, and large easel. Thanks for photocopying the handouts."

Business and technology writer Chris Joseph examines professionalism in his article, "10 Characteristics of Professionalism."[126] His characteristics include appearance, demeanor, reliability, competence, ethics, poise, phone etiquette, correspondence, organizational skills, and accountability. These points may be applied to activist and advocate grandmas. I worded the points differently to make them more personal.

Grandmas look neat and put together. When I write at home, I can sit at the computer in my pajamas. I can't wear pajamas or jeans downtown. I wear slacks because they are comfortable and add a jacket and/or scarf.

126 Chris Joseph, "Ten Characteristics of Professionalism," AAPC.

Grandmas are confident. We're not wishy-washy people. Joseph thinks professionals are polite, well-spoken, and keep calm during tense situations. I think we know how to add humor to tense situations.

Grandmas are reliable. We assess the situation, consider options, follow through, and get the job done in a timely manner. Keeping promises is a sign of reliability, according to Joseph. I think it's important to keep promises on time.

Grandmas are competent. We have a wealth of education and experience to share. Nevertheless, we keep learning and adapting because the world is a wondrous place.

Grandmas are ethical. We stand up for ethics in daily life and speak up when an organization doesn't have a code of ethics. Our behavior is our code.

Grandmas are poised most of the time. If someone is rude to us, we don't respond with rudeness. We smile and shake our heads in bewilderment. Why can't these people talk nicely?

Grandmas have phone and written etiquette. We are polite on the phone and monitor the pitch and tone of our voices. Our emails and snail mails are courteous as well.

Grandmas are organized. Planning is second nature for us. We planned for our children, are planning for our grandchildren, and planning for ourselves. Plans can always be changed to fit the situation.

Grandmas admit mistakes and move on. As Joseph writes, we "take responsibility and work to resolve the issue." In other words, we're grown-ups.

This chapter has examined advocacy and activism and given you examples of both. While I've never organized an activist group, I've organized community groups, held office in many organizations, chaired committees, and supported political candidates. Becoming an activist or advocate are individual choices and depend on your fervor. If you want to see change, work for it. When the going gets tough, keep on working. Keep this equation in your mind: Persistence + Professionalism = Success.

Leonardo da Vinci explained activism and advocacy far better than I. His words: "It had long since come to my attention that people of accomplishment rarely sat back and let things happen to them. They went out and happened to things." Go out and make things happen!

CHAPTER 12

Taking Care of Me

Essential Medical Tests
Hearing Loss
Enough Sleep
Healthy Eating and Food Preparation
Physical Activity
The Power of Quiet
The Art of Self-Kindness
Religion and Spirituality
Self-Care List

The title of this chapter may make you mutter, "I know how to take care of myself." But do you practice self-care consistently? Family responsibilities, a busy schedule, and deadlines can be distracting. Before you know it, self-care has dwindled or been forgotten. This chapter discusses basic and important self-care responsibilities that will help you be the grandma you want to be. Self-care isn't selfish; it's a necessity.

Every grandma is worthy of self-care.

This care begins with some essential medical tests.

Essential Medical Tests

Be smart about aging and get the tests you need. "10 Medical Tests Every Woman Should Have" by Lambeth Hockwald tells why you need these tests.[127] Get a bone density test to determine if your bones are getting weaker and you're at risk for osteoporosis. This is an easy test. You lie fully clothed on a table and an x-ray machine scans your spine, hips, and wrists.

A mammogram is another test that you need to have. This test is done by x-ray and your doctor will compare previous x-rays with the current ones. If a shadow (calcium deposit) appears on the x-ray you may need an MRI (magnetic resonant imaging) test.

Colonoscopy is an important test recommended for women. The American Cancer Society says screening for colorectal cancer should begin at age forty-five for those who have an average risk. Your blood pressure will be taken before the test and, if it's too high, the test will be postponed. This test involves anesthesia and you shouldn't drive afterward. Find someone to drive you home. Regular screening for colorectal cancer should continue until age seventy-five if you're in good health.

An eye exam is a must. You may have noticed vision changes and postponed a visit to the ophthalmologist. Doctors recommend annual eye exams after age sixty-five. A cataract may be developing in one or both of your eyes and an eye exam will reveal this.

Your cholesterol level needs to be tested. High cholesterol contributes to heart attack. LDL (low-density lipoprotein) is the bad cholesterol. HDL (high-density lipoprotein) is the good. If

---

127 Lambeth Hockwald, "10 Medical Tests Every Woman Should Have," *Real Simple*.

the test results concern your doctor, she or he may recommend changes in your diet and a weight loss program.

Another test you may need is a body exam for questionable moles. I had a thorough exam and no suspicious or unusual moles were found. Contact your physician immediately if you have a bleeding mole or one that changes color or shape. Removing a worrisome mole is an office procedure and takes about half an hour. The mole will be sent to a laboratory for analysis and results should be available in a week. Other tests to consider are a test for diabetes (a blood test ordered by your doctor) and an x-ray to determine if you have osteoporosis.

You can help other grandmas by reminding them to get their basic medical tests.

Despite the preventive measures, you may develop chronic illness. Chronic illnesses include diabetes, heart disease, cancer, kidney disease, osteoporosis, asthma, lupus, multiple sclerosis, obesity, and arthritis. I talked with my doctor about my arthritic hips, and she prescribed extra-strength Tylenol. This medication works for me and I depend on it.

Andrea Atkins offers ways to handle illness in her article, "6 Ways to Cope with Chronic Illness."[128] I like the way she begins her article: "Everyone gets something." Chronic illness falls into three categories, the article explains, physical, mental, and sensory (hearing and vision loss). Having chronic illness doesn't mean your life is over. I've learned to live with arthritic hips and hands (too much keyboarding), and you may live with arthritis as well.

Atkins shares some practical suggestions. The first is to stay on top of the disease. Follow your doctor's instructions, take medications as prescribed, and have check-ups when needed.

---

128 Andrea Atkins, "6 Ways to Cope with Chronic Illness," Grandparents. com.

If something doesn't feel right, make an appointment with your doctor.

I had odd feelings in my tummy for two and a half months, a feeling of something pressing on my bladder. My ovaries hurt as if I were going to have a period. These feelings led me to research the symptoms of ovarian cancer. My symptoms didn't match the symptoms I read about. However, I made an appointment with my doctor and tests showed a dark place in the middle of my tummy. The medical team reserved a day and time on the surgery calendar. It turned out I had uterine (endometrial) cancer, stage one.

"It's a good thing you listened to your body," my doctor commented. "Otherwise the outcome could have been different."

Stay in touch with your doctor. Sometimes medication dosages need to be adjusted. If a medication isn't working, contact your doctor. Be aware of the side effects of medication. For example, one of the blood pressure medications I take can cause dizziness. I never had a problem with dizziness until the day I did. I was so dizzy I put my head down to avoid passing out. This has only happened a couple of times, but I pay attention to how I'm feeling. A grandma with chronic illness has to make some trade-offs.

Medications can interact with other medications. Tell your doctor about any side effects or problems you are having. Always take your medicine as prescribed and don't stop taking it without consulting your doctor. I track my medications on a calendar. Having a written record helps me avoid the nagging question, "Did I take my meds?" This simple system works for me and will work for you. At holiday time, many businesses gift out free calendars. You can use one of these to keep track of your medication schedule.

Hearing Loss

Many grandmas are short of hearing, and I'm one of them. Perhaps your hearing isn't as good as it used to be. One third of Americans over age sixty-five have a hearing loss, and muffled sound is the first symptom.[129] Other symptoms include difficulty in following conversations, boosting the radio and television volume, and asking people to repeat themselves.

Make an appointment for a hearing test if you have any of these symptoms. Keep in mind that Medicare doesn't pay for hearing aids, and today's high-tech hearing aids are expensive. I knew I needed hearing aids when I walked into a public health meeting and saw a festive table with a cake and beverages on it. "This is for you," the public health nurse said. "We're sorry you're leaving." The farewell party was a lovely surprise. At the end of the meeting, each committee member explained why they enjoyed working with me. One member cried.

Unfortunately, I could hardly hear what people were saying. Out of necessity, I started lip reading and managed to grasp the gist of their conversations. I wondered if these kind people knew I was trying to read their lips. Happy as this occasion was, it made me nervous, and I could hardly wait until the meeting was over. Two weeks later I made an appointment for a hearing test.

Don't let hearing loss discourage you. Making just a few changes will help you hear your grandchild and other loved ones. Tell your grandchild about your hearing loss and ask her or him to tap you on the arm before speaking to you. Eliminate as much background noise as possible. Turn off the television,

---

129 Kristen Sturt, "5 Hearing Loss Symptoms," Grandparents.com.

turn off the radio, and close windows or doors if there's lots of noise outside.[130]

Enough Sleep

Without a good night's sleep, you're behind before the day begins. The lack of sleep impairs your thinking, saps your energy, and slows you down. Tasks you thought you would do quickly take longer. When the day ends, some tasks aren't done, a fact that prevents you from falling asleep. Worry may awaken you in the night. Going to bed earlier doesn't guarantee a good night's sleep. Restorative sleep hinges on many factors.

Ethan Green, founder of No Sleepless Nights and a former insomniac, thinks you need to prepare for sleep.[131] In his article, "A Bedtime Routine for Adults: 10 Calming Activities," he says a routine can work wonders. Before you go to bed, take a half hour or an hour to slow your thoughts and wind down physically. This is a time to calm an overactive mind, do the last planning of the day, and avoid overstimulating activities. You're the only one who knows how much unwinding time you need.

Unwinding means different things to different people. For Green, it means turning off electronic devices—television, computer, mobile phone, games console, or tablet. This calms his mind.

I used to watch late-night television news to get the weather forecast. Now I often skip the news and turn to the weather. Reducing noise is on my unwinding list. Because I have absolute

---

130 "Tips for Parents and Grandparents with Hearing Loss," Hearing Aid Associates.
131 Ethan Green, "A Bedtime Routine for Adults: 10 Calming Activities," No Sleepless Nights.

pitch, noise distracts me. My mind says, "Oh, that was a B flat." This happens while I'm working at the computer when I hear music on television, or a car driving by. John spends his days in a wheelchair, reading, listening to the radio, and watching television, which blares all day. Before bedtime, I ask him to turn down the volume and/or activate the television caption feature.

A busy mind can stay busy all night. Prescribed medications, breathing exercises, and mindfulness help to slow your mind. Diaphragm breathing (also called conscious breathing) is helpful. This isn't the same as chest breathing, which uses muscles in the upper chest. Mayo Clinic Registered Nurse Laura Petersen tells how do to diaphragmatic breathing in her article "Decrease Stress by Using Your Breath."[132]

Before you begin, find a comfortable position and close your eyes. Place one hand on your tummy just below your belly button and the other on your chest. Take air in through your nose and let it out through your mouth. Feel the rise and fall of your chest as you do this. Continue diaphragmatic breathing for several minutes. Once you've gotten used to this type of breathing, you can do it without involving your hands.

Having my blood pressure taken makes me anxious, and I do diaphragmatic breathing during the test to calm myself. I also use it before I give a talk to a community group or appear on radio and television.

Green also recommends reading a good book in bed. Listening to music may also be calming.[133] Some people listen to recordings of waves on a beach or rain on a roof. I particularly liked Green's fifth idea, writing down worries and reminders.

---

132 Laura Peterson, "Decrease Stress by Using Your Breath," Mayo Clinic.
133 Ethan Green, "A Bedtime Routine for Adults: 10 Calming Activities," No Sleepless Nights.

Doing so allows you to relax because you know you won't forget anything the next day.

Drinking a relaxing beverage, such as tea, is another idea. Avoid alcohol, which wakes you up later, and caffeine, which keeps you awake. Turning the thermostat to a lower temperature promotes sleep. Most people take twenty to thirty minutes to fall asleep, Green notes. Get up if you've been tossing and turning for hours. Go to another room with minimal lighting, repeat some of your routine, and go back to bed.

Although I've read many articles about sleep, none of them talked about waking up from a dream and acting on it. Once I dreamed about popcorn. I dream in color and, while I could see the yellow popcorn, I couldn't smell it or taste it. When I woke up, I had an overwhelming yearning for real popcorn. Slowly, carefully, I eased from the bed without waking John, went to the kitchen, found the electric skillet, popped a batch of corn, and ate it all. Then I went back to bed.

I still can't believe I did this and have never done it again. The exceptions are when my mind tells me something in my sleep, like adding a resource to a bibliography.

Napping is a good way to catch up on sleep. You need to do it carefully, however. Whether I nap or not depends on when I wake up. In the summer, I often wake up at four in the morning. Although I try to stay in bed, it rarely works. Getting up so early throws off the timing of the day and by ten a.m., I'm ready for lunch. Around 12:30 p.m. I start to drag and fall asleep at the computer, so I take a nap.

Mayo Clinic lists the benefits of napping in a website article, "Napping: Do's and Don't for Healthy Adults."[134] Relaxation, less fatigue, alertness, improved mood, better reaction time, and

---

134 "Napping: Do's and Dont's for Healthy Adults," Mayo Clinic.

memory are some of the benefits. I also lie down (and usually fall asleep) to relieve pain in my arthritic hips. A nap should be about thirty minutes long. Longer naps can make you groggy and disoriented, which makes it harder to sleep at night. If a young grandchild takes a nap, you could take one at the same time.

Healthy Eating and Food Preparation

Healthy eating is the next point on my self-care list. Breakfast is fuel for the day and, therefore, the most important meal of the day. Many of us have turned breakfast into a sugar festival: sugary juice, sugary cereal, sugary donuts, breakfast cookies, and waffles loaded with sugary syrup. I plead guilty to all these things. Don't ask me why, because I don't know why, but I've been craving donuts lately. After succumbing to this craving for two weeks, I pulled myself together and returned to eating healthy breakfasts.

The *Real Simple* website shares some innovative breakfast ideas and recipes in its article, "18 fast, Healthy Breakfast Ideas."[135] Some ideas that caught my attention: scrambled eggs with beans, tomatoes, and pesto; yogurt and fruit parfait; a quinoa breakfast bowl; and a peanut butter waffle. Egg in a Hole is one of my favorite breakfasts. This recipe has dozens of names, among them Toad in a Hole, Circus Eggs, Sunshine Eggs, Bull's Eye, and Spit in the Eye.

The basic recipe for Egg in the Hole only has five ingredients: bread, butter, egg, salt and pepper. Your grandchild can cut circles out of the bread with a biscuit cutter or cookie cutter. A heart-shaped cookie cutter would be fun. Then you butter the

---

135 "18 Fast, Healthy Breakfast Ideas," *Real Simple*.

bread and the hole and cook them in butter. Add some more butter to the pan—use a non-stick pan to avoid problems—flip the bread slice and crack an egg into the hole. For added flavor, I sprinkle a tablespoon of low-fat shredded Cheddar, Parmesan, or Mexican cheese blend over the cooked egg. A teenage grandchild could make this breakfast for everyone.

The US government "Choose My Plate" website can help you and your grandchild make smart food choices. The President's Council on Sports, Fitness & Nutrition is another helpful website. Its article, "Eating Healthy Eating Goals" says small changes can make big differences in health.

Often grandmas in my age group know about healthy eating and aren't looking for more information. We need motivation. I'm working on eating more vegetables and fruits. My mother developed diabetes late in life and I don't want to repeat her history. Hopefully, the small changes I'm making will help me lose a few pounds.

Carrots are my go-to snack. I also snack on fruit. I'm pushing fruits and vegetables at all meals. Usually I have three fruits for breakfast: two servings of sugar-free cranberry juice and one serving of fruit. The fruit may be cantaloupe, strawberries, blueberries, or raspberries. Fruit is paired with protein, such as half an English muffin with peanut butter. Drinking flavored, zero-calorie water helps me stay hydrated. I also serve meals on smaller plates.

Many dietitians recommend keeping a food diary, a written record of what you ate and when you ate it. This helps you identify eating patterns. I'm guilty of thrifty eating—gobbling the last bite of food on a plate because we paid for it. Other reasons for weight gain include depression, medications, slow gut, missing nutrients (magnesium, Vitamin D deficiency), knee or hip pain, and aging.[136]

Unless you're the queen of take out, you know your way around a kitchen and how to store and prepare food properly. You may not know about recent findings from the US Department of Agriculture's Department of Food Safety. Rinsing hands under warm water doesn't clean them. You are supposed to wash your hands with soap and water for twenty seconds before handling food, after preparing food, and after putting trash in the trash can. A grandchild should wash hands for the same amount of time.

Towels are one of the biggest health hazards in the kitchen and area home for bacteria. New research from the US Department of Agriculture identifies kitchen towels as the number one source of cross-contamination. Kitchen towels should be washed in hot water to remove bacteria and washed often.[137] I get out clean towels every morning, use them for a day, and launder them. Frequent washing protects your family (and your grandchild) from food poisoning. Paper towels should never be reused because they are sources of bacteria.[138]

Using a sponge to wash dishes is also dangerous. Denise Mann details these dangers in her article, "Germs in the Kitchen."[139] According to Mann, the kitchen harbors more germs than any other room in your house. "One single bacteria cell can become more than eight million cells in less than twenty-four hours!" she explains. These germs spread quickly and can cause cold and flu. Kitchen sponges are the number one source

---

136 The Prevention website cites other reasons for weight gain in an article by Baria Nan Cohen, "7 Weird Reasons You're Gaining Weight."
137 Amelia Kermis, "The Kitchen Towel Playbook," US Food Safety.
138 Kermis, "The Kitchen Towel Playbook," US Food Safety.
139 Denise Mann, "Germs in the Kitchen," WebMD.

of germs in an entire house according to Mann. Throw out your kitchen sponge to protect yourself, your family, and your grandchild.

Physical Activity

Regular physical activity is part of self-care. After a substantial meal you may feel like you need to walk off the calories. That's the way I feel. Regular physical activity helps to control weight and maintain a healthy weight. John and I used to be on a walking program. Today, he can walk only a few steps with a walker. Two arthritic hips make walking painful for me. I can ride a stationary bike, though, and do this twice a week at a health club. The old saying, "Use it or lose it" is true for grandmothers, and we need to keep moving.

I sit at the computer for hours—not my intention, but my reality. Once I get writing, I become so absorbed I lose track of time. Two hours may have passed before I check the time. Prolonged sitting can raise blood pressure, raise blood sugar, and cause excess fat around the waist. (I have a spare tire, or muffin top, as it's now called.) All of these are harmful to health and worse, according to Mayo Clinic, increase the risk from dying of heart disease or cancer.[140]

People who have sedentary jobs and sit at a computer for hours should take a break every thirty minutes, advises Mayo Clinic.[141] Another tip is to stand while talking on the phone. Have walking meetings instead of sitting meetings. Meeting participants may wear tags that say "Walking meeting in

140 Edward R. Laskowski, "What are the Risks of Sitting Too Much?" Mayo Clinic.
141 Laskowsi, "What are the Risks of Sitting Too Much?" Mayo Clinic.

progress" to avoid being interrupted. The tags could be stick-on name tags or laminated tags on a lanyard.

Some grandmas use desks that can be raised to standing height, allowing them to stand while they are writing or entering information in the computer. While I admire their efforts, I think standing would distract my thoughts and be tiring. No standing while writing for me. I do follow Mayo's advice and take a break every half hour.

Chair yoga is gaining in popularity. This gentle form of exercise is done while sitting in a chair or standing and/or using a chair for support. I had never heard of chair yoga until I saw an ad for it at the 125 Live Center for Active Adults in Rochester. Richard Kravetz describes this form of yoga in his article, "6 Benefits of Chair Yoga."[142] According to Kravetz, it improves strength, flexibility, and proprioception, which is the awareness of one's body in space. The exercises reduce stress and help with pain management.

I decided to try chair yoga and bought Kristin McGee's book, *Chair Yoga: Sit, Stretch, and Strengthen Your Way to a Happier, Healthier You.*[143] Without the breathing component, chair yoga would simply be stretching and calisthenics. McGee divides her book into helpful chapters: Upper Body, Face, Shoulders, Arms, and Wrists, Torso, Lower Body, Lower Back, and Standing Exercises. I like this because I can turn to the type of chair yoga I want.

Before you start exercising, McGee recommends some deep breathing exercises, including a calming breath, breath retention, and alternate breathing. I also do the type of breathing I learned when I was taking voice lessons in high school.

142 Richard Kravetz, "6 Benefits of Chair Yoga," Do You Yoga.
143 Kristin McGee, *Chair Yoga: Sit, Stretch, and Strengthen Your Way to a Happier, Healthier You* (New York: HarperCollins, 2017).

I began with ten minutes of chair yoga a day. The Sun Salutation (inhaling air, raising arms over my head, pressing palms together, and holding this position for a minute or so, is one of my favorite exercises. This involves many parts of the body: arms, hands, shoulders, and abdomen. When I'm working at the computer, I stop and do this exercise, along with torso twists. I benefited from McGee's book. It's reasonably priced, well organized, and easy to follow. Every exercise is pictured in sequence. Now chair yoga is part of my day.

One of John's physical therapists told him to exercise with hand weights and resistance bands several times a day. "It's not how long that counts," she explained, "it's the frequency that counts." *Frequency counts* has become my mantra.

You don't need to leave your home to be physically active. During the day you may stretch your arms, stretch your legs, lift soup cans instead of weights, do leg lifts while sitting in a chair, and touch your toes without bending your legs. Check with your doctor if you have problems with any of the exercises. I bought a pedometer and used it to track the "walks" I took in our kitchen. Walking thirty-five times around the perimeter of the kitchen added up to around five hundred steps.

The Power of Quiet

Daily quiet time helps me stay mentally fit. I think of this time as a recharging time, a source of mental and emotional power. In today's noisy world of loud music, loud traffic, construction sounds, and a twenty-four-hour news cycle, quiet is hard to find. Quiet is more than the absence of sound. Quiet can be the mental peace of green parkland or sitting by a meandering river.[144]

---

144 Suzanne Clores, "The Benefits of Quiet for Body, Mind and Spirit," Next Avenue.

Years ago, I had an unbelievable quiet time with my three-year-old granddaughter.

It was early morning at the family cabin. I sat in a log chair on the dock with my granddaughter in my lap. Patches of fog lingered in the forest and mist was rising from the river. We sat there silently, no words, no wiggling, and watched the current carry a few leaves and twigs downstream. Mayflies had hatched in the night and trout jumped from the water to catch them. One trout jumped up inches away from us. We heard other trout splashing in the river as they tried to catch mayflies. No birds were chirping, and I wondered if they were "sleeping in" on this foggy morning.

At the edge of our property, an eagle had built its nest on top of a Norway pine. When we canoed on the river, we often saw the eagle in its nest. That misty morning my granddaughter must have been thinking about the eagle because she jumped off my lap and called, "Eeeagle, you can fly overrrr, if you want to." Her sentence was almost a song. We smiled at each other and she came back and snuggled in my lap.

Minutes passed. Suddenly we heard a flapping sound as the eagle swooped low over the river, a couple of inches above the water, its claws poised to catch a trout. But the eagle missed the trout, made a quick turn, gained altitude, and flew back up river. My granddaughter and I looked at each other in amazement. Neither of us said a word. Spoken words would have spoiled nature's miracle.

I tried to write a children's story about the experience and failed. There were too many facets to the story—the stillness of the forest, the mist rising from the river, the jumping trout, the grandmother-grandchild bond, and the eagle who answered a little girl's call. Much as I hated to admit it, the story exceeded my ability to tell it. Yet I remember the story and it's one of the most beautiful times of my life. How can you find stillness and quiet?

Meditation is another way to find stillness, and there are several kinds of it. You can find more information online or buy a book on the subject. Counting breaths is another idea. Focus on breathing only. When your thoughts stray, visualize floating clouds on your mind and return to breathing.

Your grandchild benefits from quiet time and it gives her or him a chance to hear their self-talk. Quiet time helps a grandchild of any age, including an adult, figure things out and think creatively. The quiet times of life help your grandchild to observe what's going on. This is the beginning of mindfulness for a young grandchild and the practice of mindfulness for an older grandchild.

Quiet time doesn't mean boredom.

Your grandchild can look at books, read a novel, experiment with water colors, plant a container garden, practice cursive handwriting, write a story on the computer, make a birthday card for a friend, pet the dog, fly a kite, pick flowers and arrange them in a vase, make a friendship bracelet, try chair yoga, and a host of other things. Quiet times are revealing, productive times of life. Without quiet time I become a grumpy grandma. Be kind to yourself and add quiet time to each day.

The Art of Self-Kindness

Self-kindness doesn't just happen; you need to work at it. "40 Ways to Practice Self-Kindness" contains ideas that may appeal to you.[145] I like the idea of giving yourself flowers often. Ever

---

145 "40 Ways to Practice Self-Kindness," *Huffington Post.*

since my sister-in-law gave me an orchid, I've been fascinated by them. My sister-in-law can get orchids to bloom again. Not me. As soon as an orchid starts to wither, I buy another one. The flower shop clerk asked me who I was buying the plant for, and I answered, "It's a gift for me from me." She grinned and said that was a good idea.

For me, buying books is an act of self-kindness. John approves of this wholeheartedly because he reads the books after I've finished them. I pay for the books with points I've accumulated on a credit card. Books are important to us and we're always reading. I asked a carpenter to build book shelves across from my computer when I was building our townhome. When I need a book, I just turn around and grab it.

Another idea in the article is to take yourself out to dinner. I did this when I went to Boston to attend a college reunion. I enjoyed my dinner and glass of wine although I was alone. Thoughts of college friends, my supportive family, and John's love were my company. The last self-kindness idea is to speak the truth as you see it. While it's not always possible to be 100 percent truthful all the time, do it most of the time. This makes life less complicated.

Religion and Spirituality

I'm more of a spiritual person than a religious person and am okay with this. John's health challenges make it difficult for us to attend church. We need to schedule John's medications, dress for the weather, bring water, cough drops, and anything else that may be needed. Helping John get into our wheelchair van takes planning and skill. By the time we get to church, I'm exhausted. Although we don't get to many services, I try to watch them online and always read church publications.

Spirituality affects everything we do.

Jeffrey Dorfman writes about religion in a Forbes article, "Religion is Good for All of Us, Even Those Who Don't Follow One."[146] Attending services once or more a week adds seven years to your life, the article notes. Involving children (and grandchildren) in religion/spirituality reduces delinquency, smoking, leads to better school attendance, and increases the chances of graduating from high school. Dorfman suspects that those who believe in religion are happier.

Gratefulness and spirituality are connected. Being grateful opens many doors—the door to friendship, the door to socialization, the door to understanding, the door to closeness, the door to better health. Jamie Ducharme details the benefits of gratitude in his article, "7 Surprising Health Benefits of Gratitude."[147] Being grateful and making it part of your life makes you more patient, he writes. Gratefulness improves many relationships, including the grandma-grandchild relationship.

People who are grateful take better care of themselves. Surprisingly, Ducharme says gratitude may stop you from overeating. Evidently gratitude increases willpower and willpower may keep one from eating too much. In other words, gratitude boosts impulse control.

Gratitude gives you happiness that lasts,

Ducharme notes.

---

146 Jeffrey Dorfman, "Religion is Good for All of Us, Even Those Who Don't Follow One," *Forbes*.

147 Jamie Ducharme, "7 Surprising Health Benefits of Gratitude," *Time*.

Self-Care List

I created a self-care list to go with one of the talks I give. Though the list isn't comprehensive, you may find it helpful, and share it with other grandmothers.

- Take prescription meds as directed and *only* as directed.
- For emotional wellbeing, spend time with upbeat people.
- When you have negative thoughts, counter them with positive ones.
- Even though you have little to give, still give to others.
- There is at least one plant in my home and I enjoy caring for it.
- To keep your mind active, read and attend social functions.
- Limit television news viewing to one program a day.
- Eat a balanced diet and drink water to stay hydrated.
- Have a bedtime routine.
- Be grateful for each day.

I'm glad to be alive, to have these years with my devoted husband, to have a surviving, brilliant daughter, to have happy, successful grandchildren, a loving extended family, caring friends, and an occupation that brings me joy. From the ashes of sorrow, I created a new and satisfying life. The sources of my happiness are simple, yet it took decades to acquire them. I know who I am and what I can do. I continue to challenge myself. I'm proud of what I've accomplished. I know there is more to do. I am a work in progress and so are you.

Self-care is a gift to yourself and your family.

Deborah Doucette, author of *Raising Our Children's Children*, writes about families in the conclusion of her book.[148] Doucette and her husband adopted their granddaughter and raised her because she was part of them. We are all individuals, yet Doucette thinks we are wound together as families, communities, and as a society. Because we're connected, we need to be helpful, adaptive, assist with diversity, and value "each unique facet, in the noble work—the blessed art—of family."

You are family. Take care of yourself!

---

148 Deborah Doucette, *Raising Our Children's Children* (Plymouth, United Kingdom: Taylor Trade Publishing, 2014), 234, 315.

CHAPTER 13

Holding On and Letting Go

Time of Gracious Harvesting
I'm Holding On To . . .
I'm Letting Go Of . . .
The Right Timing
Acceptance Is Soul Work
Grandmas are Wisdomkeepers

Birthdays have a way of happening—family birthdays, grandchildren's birthdays, and your birthdays. In the blink of an eye, or so it seems, your grandchild became a young adult. Where did the years go? What do I do now? I wondered this after my granddaughter was married. John escorted her down the aisle in his wheelchair. My granddaughter held onto his arm as if he were walking beside her instead of in a wheelchair, a sight that made me cry.

John and I had done what grandparents are supposed to do: love and protect our grandchildren. We had gotten the twins across many finish lines: high school graduations, college choices, college graduations, and applying for jobs. Some days I find it difficult to believe the twins are adults. In his poem "For Old Age," Irish priest and poet John O'Donohue describes aging as a time for gracious harvesting.[149] This is the time to reap the many seeds we had sewn.

Time of Gracious Harvesting

I'm blessed to have been married to John for sixty-one years and have benefited from his love, intelligence, gentleness, and kindness. I have a surviving daughter who loves me and cares about me. I have amazing twin grandchildren who are creating amazing lives. The members of my extended family are a support team. Caring friends provide support as well. I have a career that challenges my intellect and brings me joy.

Take time to enjoy your harvest. Though harvest times occur all through life, the biggest harvest comes with age and being a grandma.

What seeds did you plant? What crops have you harvested? If you're a visual learner, as I am, you may wish to make a list of what you have harvested.

Gracious harvesting can be a bountiful time.

Yet it's a time to let go of some things and hold on to others. Take a big breath because making these decisions requires acceptance and courage.

Identifying the things I wanted to hold on to took me about a week. I was surprised at the list and realized the points were the foundation of my life.

---

149 John O'Donohue, *To Bless the Space Between Us: A Book of Blessings* (New York: Doubleday, 2008), 71.

I'm Holding On To . . .

I'm holding on to family gatherings. When schedules permit, the members of my extended family get together for dinner. My brother-in-law and sister-in-law live on the next block, and we often get together for dinner. These are wonderful, informal times and we talk about everything, the books we've read, the importance of a local newspaper, new construction projects, and modern-day politics (groan). Family get-togethers keep us connected.

I'm holding on to learning. Research is built into a writer's life. While I'm searching the Internet for information or scrolling through Amazon books, I always find something that grabs my attention. Research leads me in new directions, and the information I find becomes part of a book or the seeds for a new one. Learning keeps my mind active. Without learning, the day doesn't seem normal, and this throws me off balance.

I'm holding on to writing and have more ideas than I can pursue. Winnowing these ideas takes time. After I've shortened the list, I check published books to see if someone has already written on the topic. If they have, I determine if I have a different slant. I think about the marketability of the idea. I think about possible titles. I look for potential cover photos even though I haven't written a word. Writing keeps my mental gears working and helps me figure out life.

I'm holding on to speaking. Unlike some authors, who are terrified of speaking, I enjoy it, and am always looking for the next "gig." Preparing a talk or workshop intrigues me: determine the title, identify key points, write the talk, create handouts, practice the talk, time the talk, and give it. Churches, senior citizen groups, and service organizations ask me to speak.

I'm grateful for the invitations. Giving talks and workshops keeps my media skills sharp.

I'm holding on to courtesy. The other day I went to the drive-through bank. I sent the capsule to the teller. She opened it, read the name on my check and asked, "Hi Harriet. So how's it going today?" This woman was a stranger to me and I was a stranger to her. While I appreciate her friendliness, I would have preferred Ms. Hodgson. Many younger people, (the text-messaging generation), don't understand courtesy, and treat real life like Facebook. I answered her question with one word, "good," added "Thanks for your help," and drove away.

I'm holding on to healthy living. Although I have some health issues, I can't let them take over my life. For John's sake, and my own sake, I need to eat healthy and have regular physical activity. Since I'm human, sometimes I stray from the healthy living path, but I always return to it. As previously described, I've added more physical activity to my daily schedule. Hopefully, physical activity and healthy eating will help me lose a few pounds.

I'm holding on to friends. As I get older, each friend becomes more precious. Being John's primary caregiver makes it difficult to connect with friends. I have few social contacts and am active in one or two organizations. At Christmas time I host a potluck luncheon for friends. I answer email messages and Facebook messages immediately. Tragedy has taught me who my real friends are, and I'm grateful for them.

I'm holding on to giving. When people ask me to write something for them, I'm glad to do it. Mentoring other authors is something else I do. John and I donate to organizations that are meaningful to us. Giving someone an unexpected gift brings me joy. My gifts, such as blooming iris in a bud vase, aren't expensive, but they are thoughtful. Cooking is love and giving people food brings me joy. I have dozens of excellent biscotti recipes, and often give it to people for Christmas.

I'm holding on to the moment. John and I know these days with each other are precious. Because our days are numbered, we say "I love you" every day. We talk about the trips we took together, the funny things that happened to us, and our amazing grandchildren. We talk about his paraplegia and how it affected his life. We talk about love and how it continues to grow. Marrying John changed my life and made me a better person. If I hadn't married him I would be a different person, and I've often told him this.

I'm holding on to myself. As I approach the end of life, I know who I am and like this person. Becoming this person has taken me eighty-three years. Now that I've found her, I'm keeping her. Anger, arguments, resentment, criticism, whatever the ammunition may be, I won't abandon myself. If I disagree with someone, I thank them for sharing their ideas, gently state my beliefs, or I remain silent.

Life is too precious to waste on arguments and vitriol.

What are you holding on to? Think about how you will sustain these things. Other members of the Grandma Force are sources of help. Ask about their priorities and what they are focusing on now.

I'm Letting Go Of . . .

I'm letting go of corrosive people. You know who they are—the ones who always have bad news, complain constantly, and are short on solutions. Corrosive people drag others down. When I meet a corrosive person, I hear the anger in their voices and the words they use. Life is complicated enough without corrosive people, and I try to avoid them. Corrosive people are a waste of time and I don't have time to waste.

Letting go can be voluntary or involuntary. Although I let go of many things, my letting go was minimal compared to John's losses. Becoming paraplegic (not being able to use his lower body) forced John to let go of fly fishing in mountain streams and hunting with family members. He let go of our neighborhood walking program. John let go of driving, a sign of independence. John let go of contact with colleagues because the meeting place isn't really wheelchair friendly, or the elevator is too small for his electric wheelchair. Consequently, John feels left out and isolated.

John let go of travel dreams. His wheelchair is too large for a plane aisle. An airline wheelchair wouldn't work because he wouldn't be able to transfer from the chair to his assigned seat. Using a transfer board would take time and slow the loading process. If we flew somewhere, we would have to ship his wheelchair, an add-on expense. We worry about the wheelchair getting damaged or arriving late. Staying home is the easier choice for us.

John let go of modesty. There is no modesty when a paid caregiver comes each morning to get him up. He gave up on modesty the night I drove him to the hospital. However, John didn't let go of dignity, and his caregivers know this. The caregivers enjoy talking with John, and many have said they learn from him. I am constantly amazed at his positive attitude, cheerfulness, and sheer joy at being alive. "I've practiced dying three times," he has often said. "And here I am with you."

We let go of sleeping in the same bed, and it was painful. John's room is set up like a hospital room and he sleeps in a hospital bed. His room is at the back of our townhome. My room is at the front. Fortunately, if he called for help, I could hear him. I sleep in our old four-poster bed. When I'm asleep, I unconsciously move toward his side of the bed because I miss snuggling up to him after a bad dream, putting my arm around him, and finding comfort in closeness.

The Right Timing

Letting go doesn't happen all at once. It is a process and the pace of the process depends on you. You may have let go of many things and are working on letting go of others. When is it time to let go? That's a hard question to answer and you want to get it right.

Therese J. Borchard describes this process in her article "7 Ways to Let Go."[150] The trick of letting go is finding the right timing. If you let go too soon, the process is harder and takes longer. If you let go too late, your relationship may "spoil," according to the article. Finding the right time to let go requires honesty and introspection.

When the time came to let go of the twins, I trusted my instincts. Over the years, my instincts have proven to be reliable (at times surprisingly so). Letting go of the twins began the day they left for college. This was a hard day for me because I was still in protective mode.

While I wanted to protect them in college, I couldn't, and had to trust the twins' instincts. I read a blog post about a mother who was reluctant to let go when her child left for college. She jokingly suggested sending him with a life-size cutout of herself for his dorm room. The problem with letting go of a college student is that they come home again for holidays and

---

150 Therese J. Borchard, "7 Ways to Let Go," Psych Central.

summer vacations. Everything seems normal for a while, like the refrigerator door opening and closing constantly, and noisy kids coming and going. Then, just when you're used to it, the student returns to college.

When the twins came to live with us, I went back to fixing meals for four. After the twins moved out, I continued to prepare meals for four. This was an unconscious response. My subconscious mind couldn't accept the fact that the twins were gone. "There are only two of us," I kept telling myself, and then I would fix too much food again. Some might say I was creating a "new normal," yet life didn't seem normal.

We had become a grandfamily. I wanted life to stay the same, and this wasn't possible. The twins were young adults and, as their grandmother, my job was to let them go. We could still be a grandfamily, only in different ways. Finding the ways took more time than I anticipated. Painful as it was, I had to accept the fact that life had changed significantly. Coming to terms with this required truthfulness, patience, and introspection.

Acceptance Is Soul Work

Once I made up my mind to let go of the twins, I kept at it. Since I wasn't the twins' guardian any more, I resumed the role of loving grandmother and it felt comfortable. I would give advice only when asked. I would comfort and support the twins when necessary. I would encourage the twins' pursuits. I would applaud their accomplishments. I would be their cheerleader, minus the pom-poms. (I'm not the pom-pom type.) Acceptance takes time and soul work.

In addition to letting go of the twins, I let go of my former self-image as a young, energetic, thin person. That person was gone. I let go of some expectations too, such as writing more books and articles. I'll be happy if I write one more book. Because acceptance is a positive word, it can sound easy to inexperienced people. But acceptance is a complex series of emotions. Like the country song croons, you take three steps forward and two steps back. Just when you think you've accepted something, it can come back and surprise you.

Licensed therapist Joseph Wilner describes the steps to acceptance in his article, "5 Keys to Accepting What You Can't Change."[151] Cutting ties with the past is one step. The past is a reminder of the mistakes you've made and the losses you've suffered. Letting go has many benefits, Wilner explains, and they include developing a positive attitude, stress reduction, more energy, using change to your advantage, an attitude of gratitude, and more compassion.

How can you find acceptance? The past can't be changed, so you may as well leave it in the past. You can choose to remember happy times, however. While you have many coping skills, such as gathering facts before you reach a conclusion, adding to these skills may be helpful. Keep your emotions in check as you do this, Wilner advises. To care for the twins, I had to keep my feelings contained and delay some of them.

The twins needed me then, with no strings attached, and they needed my total attention, which meant John got less of it. John agreed with this approach. We focused our attention on the twins and put our faith in all the years we had been married.

Wilner thinks acceptance needs to be meaningful. Some of the worst things that happen to us evolve into life-changing personal growth. This was true of my relationship with the twins and recovering from multiple losses. Instead of allowing grief to take over my life, I put my emotional pain into writing

---

151 Joseph Wilner, "5 Keys to Accepting What You Can't Change," You Have a Calling.

about grief healing. This writing helped me and, hopefully, those who read my work. Focusing on creativity can help you achieve acceptance.

Helen's death was the greatest acceptance challenge I ever faced. The death of a child is the worst loss anyone can experience. Only those who have lost a child can understand my loss. I have accepted Helen's death and learned to live with it. For me, acceptance is a powerful emotion. I survived the worst loss a mother can have, am still standing, still working, and still with the man I adore. We survived Helen's death together and guided her precious twins with love.

Grandmas Are Wisdomkeepers

Wisdomkeepers: Meetings with Native American Spiritual Elders by Steve Wall and Harvey Arden has been on our book shelf for years.[152] I love the title. The word *wisdomkeepers* made me think of the Grandma Force.

The grandmothers of the world are wisdomkeepers.

We know the family history, the struggles family members experienced, and how they overcame these struggles. We know about different personalities and the roles family members adopt within families, such as the clown. Family members may switch roles and we've seen this too.

"I love the way you and Dad care for each other," my daughter commented. "When Dad is upset, you are calm. When you're upset, Dad is calm. You balance each other."

Experience, observations, and life-long learning make

---

152 Steve Wall and Harvey Arden, *Wisdomkeepers: Meetings with Native American Spiritual Elders* (Hillsboro, OR: Beyond Words Publishing, 1990).

grandmothers wise. Some grandmothers wanted to preserve wisdom and literacy.

Paola Gianturco, author of *Grandmother Power: A Global Phenomenon*, writes about preserving literacy in a chapter about Argentinian grandmothers.[153] In 1976 Argentina was going through a period of strife and the government burned books. Newspaper offices were bombed. Some journalists were imprisoned, tortured, and murdered. Other journalists disappeared, never to be seen again. Although the literacy rate was 97 percent, Argentinians stopped reading because the government was watching. Nobody was prepared for thousands of grandmothers to come to the rescue.

Mempo Girdinelli, an Argentinian author with forty books to his credit, moved to Mexico to escape the government.[154] He stayed for nine years and finally returned to his country. To get people reading again, he started a reading foundation and donated ten thousand of his own books to it. After he married journalist Natalia Porta Lopez, she became the coordinator of a unique program—The Story Telling Grandmothers. "This is our secret formula," explained Ms. Girdinelli. "Affection plus high-quality literature equals children who read."

These grandmothers changed Argentina, and, thanks to them, thousands of children are reading today.

The grandmothers of the world aren't merely aging, they are aging with dignity and purpose. Experts describe this as "aging well." Anne Tergesen writes about the stereotypes of aging in a *Wall Street Journal* article, "To Age Well, Change How You

---

153 Paola Gianturco, *Grandma Power: A Global Phenomenon*. Brooklyn, New York: powerHouseBooks, 2012, p. 117-119.
154 Marciel Drazer, "Storytelling Grandmothers' Spark Interest in Reading," Inter Press Agency Service News Agency.

Feel About Aging."[155] Stereotypes about aging are pervasive in the US, Tergesen notes, and many stereotypes are negative. To counter negativity, we need to sort aging myths from facts. As she writes, "The key is to hold both positive and negative in balance and really understand and own the aging process."

> The grandmother role may be more
> powerful than you realize,

powerful enough to change society, and powerful enough to change you. Members of the Grandma Force are owning aging every day. Aging is our banner and we carry it proudly. The passing years have made us stronger. We are resolute, wise, and using our age for good.

---

155 Tergesen, Anne, "To Age Well, Change How You Feel About Aging," *Wall Street Journal*.

CHAPTER 14

Conclusion

Learning from other cultures can help members of the Grandma Force be more creative, effective, and efficient. What worked for a grandma in a far-off country may work for you. It may be time for Western culture to adopt the beliefs of other cultures when it comes to aging. Western cultures have turned youth into a fetish and think of aging as shameful.[156] The physical signs of aging are distasteful for many younger people and they may use "old man" in a negative way. But in Greece, "old man" is a complimentary term.

> Age is associated with wisdom and
> worthy of respect in many cultures.

Native American cultures respect their elders and see death as part of life. I respect this concept and believe it.

Koreans highly respect their elders, and this comes from Confucianism, according to the article. The younger members of the family are expected to care for the older members. Families have huge celebrations for an elder's sixtieth and seventieth birthdays. In fact, adult children celebrate their parents' "passage into old age."

Chinese families believe that respecting elders is the high-

156 "7 Cultures That Celebrate Aging and Respect Their Elders," *Huffington Post*.

est virtue. This also comes from Confucianism. Though the westernization of some families has diminished some of these values, adult children are still expected to care for aging parents. Putting an aging mother or father in a nursing home is a dishonorable act.

Indians respect the elderly, and families tend to live in units. Elders are the heads of these family units. When a family is mulling over a decision, especially about money or a wedding, the elders are consulted. Disrespecting elders or sending them to a nursing home carries a social stigma, the article notes.

The African American culture views aging as a "natural rhythm of life." When a family member dies, the ceremony is a combination of sorrow and celebration.

Fortunately, the negative views of aging that many Westerners have are shifting, and people are seeing the positives of aging. Terry Fulmer and Drew Volmert write about this shift in "Reframing Aging: Growing 'Old at Heart.'"[157] Rather than describing aging as a battle, a new phrase—building momentum—has evolved. This finding comes from research by Frame Works, the John A. Hartford Foundation, eight other foundations, and aging organizations.

More than 10,000 people participated in the research. The phrase "building momentum" was popular with many because it is positive. The word "building" implies action, and the word "momentum" implies progress. "Research shows the metaphor's power," Fulmer and Volmert explain. I hadn't heard of "building momentum" before, but like it.

A positive attitude can prolong your life,

---

157 Terry Fulmer and Drew Volmert, "Reframing Aging: Growing 'Old at Heart,'" *Stanford Social Innovation Review.*

according to recent research findings. Melinda Beck makes this point in her article, "Starting to Feel Older? New Studies Show Attitude Can Be Critical."[158] Healthy behavior can turn into a self-fulfilling prophecy, Beck explains. People who think they can remain active do so and take better care of themselves, and consequently live longer. But people who think aging automatically means infirmity and illness may not practice self-care, and deteriorate physically.

The National Council on Aging conducted a survey of older adults in 2015. It surveyed 1,650 people by phone, including samples of Americans 60 years old and older and professionals who work with them. To stay mentally sharp, older adults and professionals agreed healthy eating and regular physical activity were important. Some felt keeping a positive attitude was their number one priority. Forty-two percent of those surveyed felt they were prepared for aging. Only 10 percent of the professionals surveyed felt older adults were really prepared for it.

You may be unsure of your feelings on aging. Sometimes my acceptance fades when I hit a roadblock. For example, I took John to Mayo Clinic for a follow-up appointment. He left the doctor's office and was headed for the elevator when his wheelchair quit. There was no power and I couldn't push the wheelchair because it was so heavy. What a dilemma! My daughter had come with us and called the local wheelchair store on her cell phone. The store dispatched two technicians and they arrived within fifteen minutes.

The wheelchair mechanic told us the power system had failed. He offered to install a used power pack at the shop until the new one arrived. Unfortunately, the power pack wasn't

---

158 Melinda Beck, "Starting to Feel Older? Two Studies Show Attitude Can Be Critical," Health Matters.

covered by insurance and cost more than $1,000. Days like this make me wonder about aging, caregiving, and staying in our townhome, but my insecurity is short-lived. Living in our townhome is the most economical option for us. To cover our bases, we signed up for two assisted living communities and paid the deposits. Visit the National Council on Aging website[159] to learn more about aging.

Whether you're ready or not, as each year passes, we grow older and continue to craft our own legacy.

A grandmother's legacy begins with love.

Resent research suggests that a close grandparent-grandchild relationship has distinct health benefits. *Boston Globe* journalist Ami Albernas thinks these benefits include less depression, wisdom passed from one generation to the next, fewer emotional and behavioral problems in children, and an historical perspective on life.[160] "These relationships also helped to reduce the adverse impacts of experiences such as parent breakups and being bullied," Albernas notes. There's more to this story.

Grandparents are reliable resources for grandchildren. They foster social skills, provide emotional support, help with schoolwork, teach acceptance, and draw family members closer together.[161] Involved grandparents, especially grandmas, can

---

159 On the website, you can take "The United States of Aging" survey, https://www.ncoa.org/news/resources-for-reporters/usoa-survey. You may also take the World Health Organization's "Aging Attitudes Quiz" on www.who.int. After you've found the website, find the title of the quiz in the box beneath the description.
160 Albernaz, Ami, "Study: Close Grandparent-Grandchild Relationships Have Healthy Benefits," *Boston Globe*.benefits
161 Lindsay Bragg, "Study: Grandparents Have Important Influence in Children's Lives." *Daily Universe*.

bring calmness and stability to their families. More importantly, we can help family members respond to and survive the crises they encounter. These benefits are important in the age of the nuclear family.

No doubt about it, we accomplish more when we work together. Stay in touch with other grandmas. If you joined an online community, post on it and check the comments that may appear after your post. Reply to the comments and work on establishing a relationship with other grandmas. Back and forth emails can help you get to know each other and your individual strengths. You may develop a working relationship with a website member. Partnering with another grandma doesn't need to be a formal arrangement.

Many formal organizations for grandmothers exist already. I'm talking about a casual approach. We can make people aware of grandmothers' volunteer efforts. We can demonstrate our willingness to help. We can share our skills, education,

and experience. We can show we are dependable, reliable, and smart—life smart and intellectually smart.

Joseph Stromberg details the importance of grandmas in his article, "New Evidence that Grandmothers Were Crucial for Human Evolution."[162] Stromberg writes about the work of University of Utah anthropologist Kristen Hawkes. She came up with something called the "grandmother hypothesis" in 1997. Hawkes and co-authors Peter Kim and James Coxworth used a computer simulation to propose that ancient grandmothers helped to collect food and feed their grandchildren to enable fertile women to have more children. In other words, grandmothers were supplementary caregivers. This theory

162 Joseph Stromberg, "New Evidence That Grandmothers Were Crucial for Human Evolution," *Smithsonian.*

helps to explain menopause, according to the researchers. Lacking menopause, older women would continue to have children and mother them. Children would be dependent on their mothers to survive.

The grandmother role of primitive women helped humans develop "a whole array of social capacities that are then the foundation for the evolution of other distinctly human traits, including pair bonding, bigger brains, learning new skills, and our tendency for cooperation," Hawkes is quoted as saying.[163]

Loving grandmothers have existed for centuries. I can picture a grandmother from years ago, feeding her grandchildren, wiping their chins, and cleaning their hands while the mother takes care of a newborn baby. I can picture a family huddled around a firepit for warmth. Grandmothers have been a key to survival for centuries and are key to the survival of modern families today. Something surprising has happened in recent years.

Young parents, whose parents have died, are looking for replacement grandparents. Donnie Davis tells about the trend in her article, "Parentless Parents Need Surrogate Grandparents."[164] Founder of the GAGA Sisterhood, Davis received requests from two young mothers looking for grandparents to "adopt." She contacted the mothers and asked for more information. They were looking for surrogate grandparents and people with grandmotherly wisdom. In her blog, Davis asked if anyone knew of an organization for surrogate parents, and if readers would be interested in doing this.

At the end of her blog she says a new organization, Surrogate

---

163 Stromberg, "New Evidence That Grandmothers Were Crucial for Human Evolution," *Smithsonian*.
164 Donnie Davis, "Parentless Parents Need Surrogate Grandparents," GAGA Sisterhood.

Grandparents of the USA, had been launched. The comments that follow Davis's post are fascinating. One person said she was surrogate grandmother to her deceased best friend's children and recommended the role to "anyone out there who needs a reason to stay young."

Another woman said she and her husband were childless and would be willing to serve as surrogate grandparents "to share life, learning and laughter." A man said he had missed the joys and challenges of parenthood and it wasn't too late to be a surrogate grandfather for a child. Apparently there are hundreds, perhaps thousands, of grandparents willing to serve as surrogate grandparents for children.

Randy Lilleston writes about surrogate grandparents in his article, "For Surrogate Grandparents, the Ties Still Bind."[165] He says the Surrogate Grandparents of the USA already had 2,500 members although it was only two years old.

Grandmas have so much to share. You may decide to organize a group of five grandmas and work on finding solutions for community problems. Five dedicated grandmas can make a difference. Twenty-five grandmas can make a big difference; 125 grandmas can make a huge difference. Best-selling novelist Frederik Backman compares having a grandmother to having a personal army.[166] The army is always ready, he says, even if a grandchild is wrong, and especially if a grandchild is wrong. "A grandmother is both a sword and a shield," he writes.

You can be your grandchild's sword and shield. Although the Grandma Force doesn't have a formal organization with dues or a logo or a website, we have each other. And this is our

---

165 Lilleston, Randy, "For Surrogate Grandparents, the Ties Still Bind," AARP.
166 Frederick Backman, *My Grandmother Asked Me to Tell You She's Sorry* (New York, NY: Atria Books, 2015).

strength. Singly and together, grandmas can love, protect, and nurture grandchildren around the world. Grandmas are needed more than ever, and we need you in the Grandma Force. There is no better time. There is no greater calling. We are grandmas!

BIBLIOGRAPHY

Adcox, Susan. "Groundbreaking Studies About Grandparents." *Resources for Grandparents Raising Grandchildren* (website).

Albernaz, Ami. "Study: Close Grandparent-Grandchild Relationships Have Healthy Benefits," *Boston Globe*, December 13, 2015.

American Grandparents Association. "Surprising Facts About Grandparents." *Food and Leisure.* http://www.grandparents.com/food-and-leisure/did-you-know/surprising-facts-about-grandparents

American Grandparents Association. "The Ultimate Guide to Grandparent Names." *Family and Relationships.* https://www.grandparents.com/family-and-relationships/grandparent-names/grandparent-names

Anderson, Jeff. "Why Grandparents Matter More than Ever." *Senior Living* (blog).

Angelica. "30 Body Languages and Their Meanings." *EnkiVeryWell* (website).

Atkins, Andrea. "6 Ways to Cope with Chronic Illness." *Grandparents.com.*

Aubel, Judi. "Grandmother Project: Involving Grandmothers to Promote Child Nutrition, Health and Development." *The Grandmother Project* (website).

Backman, Frederick. *My Grandmother Asked Me to Tell You She's Sorry.* New York, NY: Atria Books, 2015.

Barnett, Rosalind C., and Rivers, Caryl. "Why Your Grandmother is Still Working." *Psychology Today* (blog).

Basco, Monica Ramirez. "The Perfect Trap." *Psychology Today* (website). https://www.psychologytoday.com/us/articles/199905/the-perfect-trap

Beck, Melinda. "Starting to Feel Older? Two Studies Show Attitude Can Be Critical." *Health Matters* (website). https://www.wsj.com/articles/SB10001424052748704471504574445263666118226

Becker, Paula. "Knitting for Victory—World War II." *History Link* (website). http://www.historylink.org/File/5722

Ben-Joseph, Elana Pearl. "Internet Safety." *KidsHealth*. https://kidshealth.org/en/parents/net-safety.html

Birdsong, Toni. "To Skype or Not to Skype: What Parents Need to Know about Video Chat." *Securing Tomorrow* (website).

Blatner, Adam. "Belonging-Ness." *Adam Blatner* (website). Last modified June 20, 2008. http://www.blatner.com/adam/psyntbk/belongingness.html

Bollet, Felicia. "9 Crafty Ways to Display Grandkids' Art." *Grandparents.com.*

Borchard, Therese J. "7 Ways to Let Go." *PsychCentral* (blog).

Bosak, Susan V. "Grandparents Day Planning & Activity Guide." *Legacy Project* (website).

Bosak, Susan.V. "Grandparents Today." *Legacy Project* (website). http://www.legacyproject.org/guides/gptoday.html

Bosak, Susan V. *How to Build a Grandma Connection.* Whitchurch, Ontario: The Communication Project, 2000, p. 29, 68-73.

Bosak, Susan V. "Why Grandparents Are VIPs." *Legacy Project* (website). http://www.legacyproject.org/guides/gpvip.html

Bragg, Lindsay. "Study: Grandparents Have Important Influence in Children's Lives." *Daily Universe*, November 15, 2011.

Breitlinks. "Children's Genres." http://breitlinks.com/my_libmedia/children%27s_genres.htm

Brhel, Rita. "The Vital Importance of the Grandparent-Grandchild Bond." *Attached Family* (website). http://theattachedfamily.com/membersonly/?p=164

Carpenter, Lisa. "Top 6 Grandparent Guilt Trips—And How to Overcome Them." *American Grandparents Association.*

Centers for Disease Control and Prevention. "Depression is Not a Normal Part of Growing Older." https://www.cdc.gov/aging/mentalhealth/depression.htm

Centers for Disease Control and Prevention. "Why are Family Rules Important for Toddlers and Preschoolers?" https://www.cdc.gov/parents/essentials/structure/familyrules.html

Clores, Suzanne. "The Benefits of Quiet for Body, Mind and Spirit." *Next Avenue* (website). https://www.nextavenue.org/benefits-quiet-body-mind-and-spirit/

Club Industry. "Health Clubs for Children are a Growing Trend." https://www.clubindustry.com/profits/health-clubs-children-are-growing-trend

Cohen, Baria Nan. "7 Weird Reasons You are Gaining Weight." *Prevention* (website).

Collins, Jerri. "How Do I Avoid Dangerous Websites?" *LifeWire* (website). https://www.lifewire.com/avoid-dangerous-websites-3481594

Davis, Donne. "Parentless Parents Need Surrogate Grandparents." *GAGA Sisterhood* (website).

Domanico, Kelli. "The Role of Grandparents in the Modern Family." *WPRI Eyewitness News*, November 17, 2014.

Dorfman, Jeffrey. "Religion is Good for All of Us, Even Those Who Don't Follow One." *Forbes*, December 22, 2013.

Doucette, Deborah. *Raising Our Children's Children*. Plymouth, United Kingdom: Taylor Trade Publishing, 2014, p. 234, 315.

Drakakis, Helena. "Nana Café Embraces the Talents of Grandmothers." *Guardian* (website).

Drazer, Maricel. "Storytelling Grandmothers' Spark Interest in Reading." *Inter Press Agency Service News Agency*. http://www. ipsnews.net/2006/02/argentina-storytelling-grandmothers-spark-interest-in-reading/

Ducharme, Jamie. "7 Surprising Health Benefits of Gratitude." *Time*, November 20, 2017. http://time.com/5026174/health-benefits-of-gratitude/

Empowering Parents. "Grandparents and Parents Disagreeing? 11 Tips for Both of You." https://empoweringparents.com/article/grandparents-and-parents-disagreeing-11-tips-for-both-of-you/

Eyre, Linda. *Grandmothering: The Secrets to Making a Difference While Having the Time of Your Life*. Sanger, CA: Familius, 2018, p. 62-66.

Feinstein, Stu. "Letter Writing is a Lost Art. Grandparents Should Revive It." *Grandparents.com*.

Fidelity. "How Grandparents Can Help Fund College." *Viewpoints: Personal Finance*.

Fishel, Elizabeth, and Jeffrey Jensen Arnett. "Parenting Adult Children: Are You a Good Friend to Your Grown-Up Kid?" *AARP*. https://www.aarp.org/home-family/friends-family/info-04-2013/parenting-adult-children-family-relationships.html

Flynn, Kathryn. "10 Easy Ways Grandparents Can Help Pay for College." *Saving for College* (website). https://www.savingforcollege.com/articles/10-easy-ways-grandparents-can-help-pay-for-college-801

Foundations Magazine. "George Washington's Rules of Civility & Decent Behavior." *Traditions*. http://www.foundationsmag.com/civility.html

Foundation for Grandparenting. "Long-Distance Grandparenting." http://grandparenting.org/resource/long-distance- grandparenting/

Friedman, Karen. *Shut Up and Say Something: Business Communication Strategies to Overcome Challenges and Influence Listeners.* (Santa Barbara, CA: Praeger, 2010), 165.

Fritz, Joanne. "How to Write an Amazing Nonprofit Mission Statement," *Balance Small Business* (website). https://www.thebalancesmb.com/how-to-write-the-ultimate-nonprofit-mission-statement-2502262

Fulmer, Terry and Volmert, Drew, "Reframing Aging: Growing 'Old at Heart.'" *Stanford Social Innovation Review.*

GaGa Sisterhood. "How to Connect with Your Teenage Grandchild." https://www.gagasisterhood.com/2018/how-to-connect-with-your-teenage-grandchild/

Gaille, Brandon. "23 Statistics on Grandparents Raising Grandchildren." *Brandon Gaille Small Business & Marketing Advice* (website).

Gavin, Mary. "Bonding with Grandchildren." *Kids Health* (website). http://kidshealth.org/en/parents/grandparents.html

Gianturco, Paola. *Grandmother Power: A Global Phenomenon.* Brooklyn, NY: Powerhouses Books, 2012, p.8, 49-51, 117-119.

Goleman, Daniel. *Emotional Intelligence: Why It Can Matter More Than IQ.* New York: Bantam Books, 1997, p. 4, 9.

Goyer, Amy. "Grandparents in Action." *AARP*. https://www.aarp.org/online-community/people/ShowProfile.action?UID=1812&plck UserId=1912.html

Graham, Barbara. "7 Unbreakable Laws of Grandparenting." *American Grandparents Association*. https://www.grandparents.com/family-and-relationships/family-matters/barbara-graham-7-laws-of-grandparenting

Graham, Barbara. "We All Want to Help with the Kids, but No One

Wants to be Taken for Granted." *AARP*. https://www.grandparents. com/family-and-relationshps/caring-for-grandchildren/ grandmother-not-babysitter-barbara-graham

Grandmothers Advocacy Network. "Grandmothers Advocacy Network (Gran)." Homepage. http://grandmothersadvocacy.org/

GransNet. "Different Types of Grandmother." https://www.gransnet. com/grandparenting/good-granny-guide/types-of-granny

GransNet. "Taking Your Grandchildren to the Park." https://www. grandsnet.com/grandparenting/good-granny-guide/at-the-park

Goyer, Amy. "Grandparents in Action." *AARP*. https://www.aarp. org/online-community/people/showProfile.action?UID =1812&plckUserld=1912.html

Gray, Peter. "In Relationships, Respect May Be Even More Crucial than Love." *Psychology Today* (blog).

Green, Ethan. "A Bedtime Routine for Adults: 10 Calming Activities." *No Sleepless Nights* (website). https://www.nosleeplessnights.com/ sleep-hygiene/bedtime-routine-for-adults/

Grandmothers Advocacy Network. "Who are We? What Do We Do?" Homepage. http://grandmothersadvocacy.org/

Grand magazine. "Characteristics of Effective Grandparents." *Resources*.

https://www.grandmagazine.com/2012/08/effective- grandparenting/

Guertin, Amy. "List of Family Values." *Love to Know* (website). https://family.lovetoknow.com/list-family-values

Haden, Jeff, "9 Habits of People Who Build Extraordinary Relationships," *Inc.*, https://www.inc.com/jeff-haden/9-habits-of-people- who-build-extraordinary-relationships.html

Hearing Aid Associates. "Tips for Parents and Grandparents with

Hearing Loss." *Healthy Hearing.* https://www.healthyhearing.com/report/38856-Parents-hearing-loss-tips

Hockwald, Lambeth. "10 Medical Tests Every Woman Should Have." *Real Simple.* https://www.realsimple.com/health/preventative-health/10-medical-tests-ever-woman

Huffington Post. "7 Cultures That Celebrate Aging and Respected Their Elders," *Life: Wellness.* Last modified December 6, 2017. https://www.huffingtonpost.com/2014/02/25/what-other-cultures-can-teach_n_4834228.html

HuffPost. "40 Ways to Practice Self-Kindness," Kindness Blog. Last modified November 26, 2014. https://www.huffingtonpost.com/kindness-blog/40-ways-to-practice-selfk_b_5886794.html

Joseph, Chris. "Ten Characteristics of Professionalism." AAPC. https://www.aapc.com/blog/40477-10-characteristics-of-professionalism-in-the-workplace/

Kandel, Bethany. "How to Choose Your Grandparent Name: Sometimes You Pick Your Name. Sometimes It Picks You." *Grandparents.com.* http://www.grandparents.com/family-and-relationships/grandparent-names/choose-your-grandparent-name

Keller, Kristen. "73-Year-Old Grandmother Completes Her GED." *Jersey Journal,* November 6, 2017. https://www.nj.com/hudson/index.ssf/2017/11/73-year-old_grandmother_completes_her_ged.html

Kermis, Amelia. "The Kitchen Towel Playbook." *US Food Safety* (blog).

Kids Health. "Getting Involved in Kids' Online Activities." Parents. http://kidshealth.org/en/parents/net-safety.html

Kilka, Grett. "Top 10 Reasons Children Should Exercise." Education and Resources. Ace Fitness (blog). https://www.acefitness.org/education-and-resources/lifestyle/blog/6441/top-10-reasons-children-should-exercise

Kobe, Ellen. "10 Things to Know Before Building Your Little Free Library," *Milwaukee Journal Sentinel*, July 26, 2014. http://archive.jsonline.com/features/home/10-things-to-know-before-building-your-little-free-library-b99310728z1-268522622.html

Krakakis, Helena. "Nana Café Embraces the Talents of Grandmothers." *The Guardian.* https://www.theguardian.com/society/2014/jan/22/nana-cafe-embraces-talents-grandmothers

Kravetz, Richard. "6 Benefits of Chair Yoga." *Do You Yoga* (website).

Laskowski, Edward R. "What are the Risks of Sitting Too Much?" *Mayo Clinic.* https://www.mayoclinic.org/healthy-lifestyle/adult-health/expert-answers/sitting/faq-20058005

LeaMond, Nancy. *Where We Live: Communities for All Ages.* Washington, DC: AARP, 2018, p. 7.

Levenick, Denise May. "5 Family Heirlooms Heirs Actually Want to Inherit." *Family Curator* (website). https://thefamilycurator.com/top-5-family-heirlooms-they-actually-want-to-inherit/

Levitt, Shelly. "Five Things to Celebrate in New Attitudes Toward Aging." *Get Old* (website). https://www.getold.com/five-things-to-celebrate-in-new-attitudes-toward-aging

Lewis, Nina. "Skype with Grandchildren." *Grandma Ideas* (website). http://grandmaideas.com/skype-with-grandchildren

Lickerman, Alex. "Personality vs. Character," *Psychology Today* (blog).

LifeWire. "Fundamental Email Etiquette: 26 Easy Rules to Follow." https://www.lifewire.com/fundamental-email-etiquette-1171187

Lilleston, Randy. "For Surrogate Grandparents, the Ties Still Bind," *AARP.* https://www.aarp.org/home-family/friends-family/info-2017/surrogate-grandparents-benefits-fd.html

LoFrumento, Mary Ann. "Have You Bonded with Your Grandchild?" *Grandparents.com.* https://grandparents.com/grandkids/nes-grandparents/have-you-bonded-with-your-grandchild

Mann, Denise. "Germs in the Kitchen." *WebMD*. https://www.webmd. com/food-recipes/features/germs-in-kitchen#1

Mann, Jen. "10 Rules Every Grandparent should Know," *Huffington Post* (blog), January 29, 2013. https://www.huffpost.com/entry/ rules-for-grandparents_b_2569629

Manno, Michelle. "Tell Us Your Story: Blog to Support Special Needs." *Tell Us Your Story* (website). https://teach.com/blog/tell-us-your-story-blog-to-support-special-needs/

Martin, Ben. "Challenging Negative Self-Talk." *PsychCentral* (website). https://psychcentral.com/lib/challenging-negative-self-talk/

Mattel, Audrey. "The Joy of Watching Grandchildren Grow into Adults," *Catholic Herald*, March 22, 2012. http://www. madisoncatholicherald.org/grandmom/3060-grandmom.html

Maughan, Shannon. "American Academy of Pediatrics Backs Reading Aloud from Infancy," *Publishers Weekly*, June 24, 2014. https://www. publishersweekly.com/pw/by-topic/childrens/childrens-industry-news/article/63008-american-academy-of-pediatrics-backs-reading-aloud-from-infancy.html

Mayo Clinic. "Napping: Do's and Don'ts for Healthy Adults." *Healthy Lifestyle*.   https://www.mayoclinic.org/healthy-lifestyle/adult-health/in-depth/napping/at-20048319

Mayo Clinic. "Support Groups: Make Connections, Get Help." *Healthy Lifestyle*.   https://www.mayoclinic.org/healthy-lifestyle/stress-management/in-depth/support-groups/art-20044655

McGee, Kristin. *Chair Yoga: Sit, Stretch, and Strengthen Your Way to a Happier, Healthier You*. New York: HarperCollins, 2017.

Medhus, Elisa. "The Importance of a Strong Family Identity." *Struggling Teens* (website). http://www.strugglingteens.com/archives/2001/8/oe03.html

Medical Dictionary. "Myers-Briggs Type Indicator." The Free Dictionary. https://medical-dictionary.thefreedictionary.com/Myers-Briggs+Type+Indicator

Murphy, Lisa. "10 Tips for Hosting a Successful Sleepover." *Today's Parent* (website). https://www.todaysparent.com/kids/10-tips-for-successful-sleepovers/

Myers, Robert. "4 Ways to Spot and Nurture Talent in Your Child." *Child Development Institute.* https://childdevelopmentinfo.com/child-activities/4-ways-to-spot-and-nurture-talent-in-your-child/

National Council on Aging. "Older Adults and Professionals Who Support Them: What Matters Most?" *Resources for Reporters.* https://www.ncoa.org/news/resources-for-reporters/usoa-survey/infographic/

National Council on Aging. "The United States of Aging Survey." *Resources for Reporters.* https://www.ncoa.org/news/resources-for-reporters/usoa-survey

O'Donohue, John. *To Bless the Space Between Us: A Book of Blessings.* New York, NY: Doubleday, 2008, p. 48

Olds, Sally Wendkos. *Super Granny: Great Stuff to Do with Your Grandkids.* New York, NY: Sterling, 2009, p. xiv, xiii.

Omohundro, Katie. "Five Steps to Better Communication with Your Teen." *Washington Times Herald*, March 31, 2018. http://www.washtimesherald.com/comumns/five-steps-to-better-communication-with-your-teen/article_1bc64a3a-698c-53e0-9587-3ee170d64561.html

Peterson, Laura. "Decrease Stress by Using Your Breath." *Mayo Clinic.* https://www.mayoclinic.org/healthy-lifestyle-stress-management/in-depth/decrease-stress-by-using-your-breath/art-20267197

Pincus, Debbie. "Grandparents and Parents Disagreeing? 11 Tips for Both of You," *Empowering Parents* (website). https://www.empoweringparents.com/article/grandparents-and-parents-disagreeing-11-tips-for-both-of-you/

Points of Light. "12 Service Project Ideas for Kids." *Blog*. http://www.pointsoflight.org/blog/2016/08/31/12-service-project-ideas-kids

Price-Mitchell, Marilyn. "What is a Role Model? Five Qualities that Matter to Youth." *Roots of Action* (website). https://www.rootsofaction.com/role-model/

PR Newswire. "Number of Children Raised by Grandparents and Other Relatives Continues to Rise During Opioid Crisis." https://www.prnewswire.com/news-releases/number-of-children-raised-by-grandparents-and-other-relatives-continues-to-rise-during-opioid-crisis-300708200.html

Pruess, Joanna. "Why Cooking with Grandkids Matters." *Next Avenue* (website). Last modified August 9, 2012. https://www.nextavenue.org/why-cooking-with-your-grandkids-matters/

Psychology Today. "Definition of Perfectionism." *Psychology Today* (website).   https://www.psychologytoday.com/intl/basics/perfectionism

Raise Smart Kid, "Benefits of Reading to Your Child." https://www.raisesmartkid.com/all-ages/1-articles/14-the-benefits-of-reading-to-your-child

Ramnarace, Cynthia, "The Granny Nanny Phenomenon." Relationships. *AARP*. https://www.aarp.org/relationships/grandparenting/info-02-2009/the_granny_nanny_phenomenon.html

Ramsey, Dave. "Spoiling Your Grandchildren Isn't Your Right." *Dave Ramsey* (blog). https://www.daveramsey.com/blog/grandparent-giving-unspoken-secrets-you-must-know

Real Simple. "18 Fast, Healthy Breakfast Ideas." *Food recipes*. https://www.realsimple.com/food-recipes/recipe-collections-favorites/healthy-meals/breakfast-to-go

Rettew, Bill. "Grandparents, Grandchildren Learn Together at WCU." *The Mercury* (website). https://www.pottsmerc.com/news/grandparents-grandchildren-learn-together-at-wcu/article_727f6ad2-d6a3-5c63-91ce-aece5f20722e.html

Rienzi, Edna. "Helping Your Kids Give Back: 11 Fun Holiday Service Ideas for You and Your Family." *New Dream* (blog). https://newdream.org/blog/fun-holiday-service-projects-for-you-and-your-family

Roessel, Jaclyn. "Grownup Navajo: The Transformative Power of Grandmothers in Our Culture." *Aculturame* (website).

Sasson, Remez. "Achieving Success Requires Patience and Persistence." *Success Consciousness* (website). https://www.successconsciousness.com/blog/inner-strength/achieving-success-requires-patience-and-persistence/

Safe Search Kids. "Cell Phone Safety Tips." https://www.safesearchkids.com/cell-phone-safety-tips-for-tweens-and-teens/

Schreur, Jerry and Schreur, Judy. "Grandparents as Role Models." *Focus on the Family* (website). http://focusonthefamily.com/marriage/the-early-years/many-roles-of-grandparents/grandparents-as-role-models

Second Harvest Food Bank of Middle Tennessee. "Starting a Backpack Program." https://secondharvestmidtn.org/wp-content/uploads/2011/08/Starting-Your-Own-BackPack-Program.pdf

Segal, Jeanne, and Robinson, Lawrence. "How to Be a Better Grandparent." *Help Guide* (website). https://www.helpguide.org/articles/grandparenting/how-to-be-a-better-grandparent.htm#resources

Seifert, Sheila. "Age-Appropriate Chores: How to Help Kids Be Responsible." *Focus on the Family* (website). https://www.focusonthefamily.com/parenting/parenting-challenges/motivating-kids-to-clean-up/age-appropriate-chores

Sheridan, Michael. "Secret Nazi Saboteurs Invaded Long Island During World War II, M15 Documents Reveal." *New York Daily News.* http://www.nydailynews.com/new-york/secret-nazi-saboteurs-invaded-long-island-world-war-ii-mi5-documents-reveal-article-1

Spring.org. "Sense of Belonging Increases Meaningfulness of Life." *PsyBlog.* https://www.spring.org.uk/2013/10/sense-of-belonging-increases-meaningfulness-of-life.php

Spring, Kelly A. "Food Rationing and Canning in World War II," *National Women's History Museum.* https://nwhm.org/articles/food-rationing-and-canning-world-war-II

Smithsonian. "New Evidence that Grandmothers Were Crucial for Human Evolution." https://www.smithsonianmag.com/science-nature/new-evidence-that-grandmothers-were-crucial-for-human-evolution-88972191

Stahl, Lesley. "On Becoming a Grandmother." Home and Family. *AARP.* https://www.aarp.org/home-family/friends-family/info-2016/becoming-a-grandmother.html

Strom, Robert D. "Building a Theory of Grandparent Development." *Arizona State University.* http://www.public.asu.edu/~rdstrom/GPtheory.html

Stromberg, Joseph. "New Evidence That Grandmothers Were Crucial for Human Evolution." *Smithsonian.* https://www.smithsonianmag.com/science-nture/new-evidence-that-grandmothers-were-crucial-for-human-evolution-88972191/

Sturt, Kristen. "5 Hearing Loss Symptoms." *Grandparents.com.* http://www.nowuknowonline.com/profiles/blogs/5-hearing-loss-symptoms

Tabares, JoJo. "Humor: A Powerful Communication Tool?" *Parents Corner* (website). https://creation.com/humor-a-powerful-communication-tool

Tahmaseb-McConatha, Jasmin. "Learning to Be a Grandmother," *Psychology Today* (blog). https://www.psychologytoday.com/us/blog/live-long-and-prosper/201311/learning-be-grandmother

Tergesen, Anne. "To Age Well, Change How You Feel About Aging." *Wall Street Journal.* https://www.wsj.com/articles/to-age-well-change-how-you-feel-about-aging-1445220002

The National Long Distance Relationship Building Institute. "20 Activities for Grandparents to do with their Grandchildren." http://www.fambooks.com/activities.html

Tschabitscher, Heinz. "Fundamental Email Etiquette: 20 Easy Rules to Follow." *LifeWire* (website). https://www.lifewire.com/fundamental-email-etiquette-1171187

Tutorials Point. "Body Language-Open & Closed." https://www.tutorialspoint.com/

Vajda, Peter. "Emotional Intelligence or Emotional Maturity?" Management Issues. https://www.management-issues.com/opinion/6811/emotional-intelligence-or-emotional-maturity/

Wall, Steve, and Arden, Harvey. *Wisdomkeepers: Meetings with Native American Spiritual Elders*. Beyond Words Publishing, Inc.

Wallace, Meri. "Understanding Children's Emotional Needs." *Psychology Today* (blog). https://www.psychologytoday.com/us/blog/how-raise-happy-cooperative-child/201710/understanding-childrens-emotional-needs

WebMD. "Baby Talk: Communicating with Your Baby." *Parenting, Baby, Reference*. https://www.webmd.com/parenting/baby/baby-talk

Whitbourne, Susan Krauss. "Five Types of Grandparents and How They Shape Your Lives," *Psychology Today* (blog). https://www.psychologytoday.com/blog/fulfillment-any-age/201002/five-types-of-grandparents-and-how-they-shape-your-lives

Women's Center for Healing. "Grandmother Group." http://womenscenterforhealing.org/grandmother-group.html

Wright, Lexi Walters. "10 Ways to Improve Your Grade-Schooler's Communication Skills." *Understood* (website). https://www.understood.org/en/learning-attention-issues/child-learning-disabilities/communication-disorders/10-ways-to-improve-your-grade-schoolers-communication-skills

Younger, Shannon. "7 Reasons Why Reading Aloud to Older Kids is Still Very Important." *Chicago Now* (website).

Zadok, Sarah. "Grandmother = Free Babysitter." *Jewish Woman. Chabad.org.* https://www.chabad.org/theJewishWoman/article_cdo/aid/404538/jewish/Grandmother-Free-Babysitter.htm

Zero to Three. "How to Support Your Child's Communication Skills." *Resources and Services.* https://www.zerotothree.org/resources/302-how-to-support-your-child-s-communication-skills

ABOUT THE AUTHOR

Harriet Hodgson, BS, MA has been a writer for thirty-nine years. She is the author of thirty-six books and thousands of print and online articles. Hodgson is a member of the Association of Health Care Journalists, Alliance of Independent Authors, and the Minnesota Coalition for Death Education and Support. She is a contributing writer for the Open to Hope website, The Grief Toolbox website, and The Caregiver Space website.

Hodgson has appeared on more than 185 radio talk shows, including CBS Radio, and dozens of television stations, including CNN. She has also appeared on many BlogTalkRadio programs. A popular speaker, Hodgson has given presentations at public health, Alzheimer's, bereavement, and caregiving conferences.

Her work is cited in *Who's Who of American Women*, *World Who's Who of Women*, *Contemporary Authors*, and other directories. "I'm proud to be a grandmother," Hodgson said, "and proud to write about the grandmothers of the world." Hodgson lives in Rochester, Minnesota, with her husband, John. Please visit www.harriethodgson.com for more information about this busy wife, mother, grandmother, caregiver, author, and speaker.

Other Grandparenting Books
by Harriet Hodgson

According to the US Census Bureau, more than 10% of all grandparents in the nation are raising their grandkids, and the number is going up.

You may be one of these grandparents and it's a role you never expected. Willing as you are to assume this role, you have some questions. How will I find the energy for this? Is my grandchild normal? What if I "blow it?" Each day, you look for ways to make life easier.

Help has arrived. This inspiring self-help book for grandparents raising grandchildren will: Help ease your worries and guilt; Offer tips for creating a grandfamily; Give methods for improving grandparent-grandchild communication; Suggest ideas for how you can connect with your grandchild's school; Provide child development information; Recommend approaches to help your grandchild set goals; Stress the importance of having fun together; Offer ideas of how to foster your grandchild's hopes and dreams.

So, You're Raising Your Grandkids blends Harriet Hodgson's unbelievable grandparenting story with recent research and findings. It comes from her 21 years of caregiving experience, including seven years of raising her twin grandkids. Each chapter ends with What Works, proven tips for grandparents raising grandkids. At the end, you'll cheer for all the loving grandparents—including you—who are putting grandchildren first.

INDEX